Chris D. Burton

The Nightingale

A Chamber Opera in One Act
based on the tale by Hans Christian Andersen

2014

Piano/Vocal Score

Performance Notes

- ♪. = ♪ throughout the score unless specifically listed otherwise.

- Accidentals apply only to the octave represented. Accidentals apply to all notes within a measure. In recitative sections, accidentals apply until cancelled. Some courtesy accidentals may be found, but they do not overrule this.

- There are three methods of sound production throughout this work:

  - Sung music – represented by normal notation.

  - Speech-singing – represented by music without noteheads. Pitches are approximate and should follow the general contour and rhythm of the line. (see Scene 1, m. 147 on page 18)

  - Spoken dialog – represented as paragraph text written, above or directly on the staff. Though these lines may (and should) sometimes be overdramatic, do not attempt to place them on a pitch. (see page 42)

- Triangle noteheads represent approximate pitches usually at the extreme high or low of a range, i.e. a very high pitch as in a musing "hmm." (see Scene 1, m. 147 on page 12)

- Vocal lines without text are intended to be sung on nonsense syllables ("ah", "oo", "humm", etc.) that may be improvised to the singers comfort.

- Vocal lines without stems (primarily the Nightingale) are intended to be sung out of time yet relative to the shape of the noteheads surrounding them. For example, a whole-note notehead should be longer than a half-note notehead. Grace notes should each be sung clearly, not simply glossed over, but do still move at a fast rate. Much of the pace of these sections may be changed to fit the comfort of the singer.

- Sections of music that are placed in boxes are intended to be sung freely, not in time with the accompaniment. (see page 44)

- Rhythmic values within a recitative section or within a box are completely relative and may be somewhat altered for clarity of text, comfort of the singer, or similar reasons.

- The marking *Tempo* is a cancellation of *Recit* and picks up at the most recent tempo. (see Scene 1, m. 142 on page 11)

Cast List

Nightingale (N.) ....Soprano
Mechanical Nightingale (M.N.) ....Soprano
Kitchenmaid (K.) (also Spirit 1 [Sp. 1]) ......Soprano/Soubrette
Chancellor (C.) (also Spirit 2 [Sp. 2]) ....Mezzo-Soprano
Narrator (Nar.) ....Baritone
Emperor (E.)..Baritone

Instrumentation

Flute
(doubling Piccolo, C Flute, and Alto Flute)

Cello

Mallet Percussion (percussion 1)
(Vibraphone (mallets and bass bow), Marimba*, Triangle*)

Auxiliary Percussion (percussion 2)
(Set of 3 cymbals (yarn mallets and wire brushes), Marimba* (mallets and bass bow),
Glockenspiel, Large Tom (or Floor Tom or Tenor drum),Triangle*, Vibraslap, Ocean
Drum or Rain Stick, Lions' Roar or Cuica, Guiro, Ratchet)

*percussion instruments to be shared

Table of Contents

The Nightingale
An Opera in One Act
based on the tale by Hans Christian Andersen

Scene 1

The Imperial Palace / The Forest
Narrator, Nightingale, Emperor, Chancellor, Kitchenmaid

The imperial throne-room should be set up on one side of the stage with the forest
on the other. The narrator exists outside of these spaces but interacts with both
as he addresses them. The Nightingale may enter and leave the forest as needed.
The emperor and chancellor may either be sitting in the throne room or may enter on cue.

Music and Libretto:
Chris D. Burton (ASCAP)

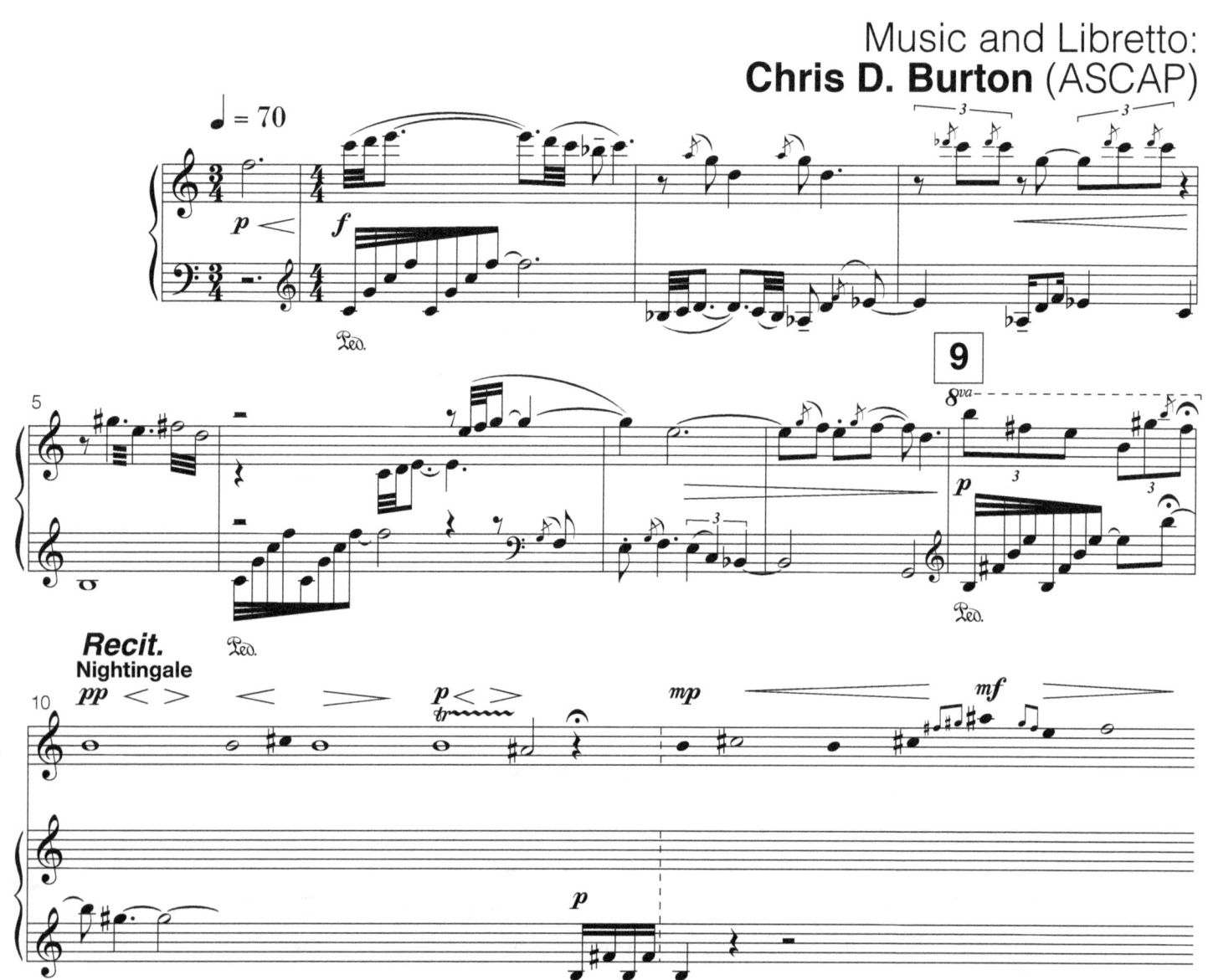

Contact the composer to organize a performance
www.ChrisDBurton.com

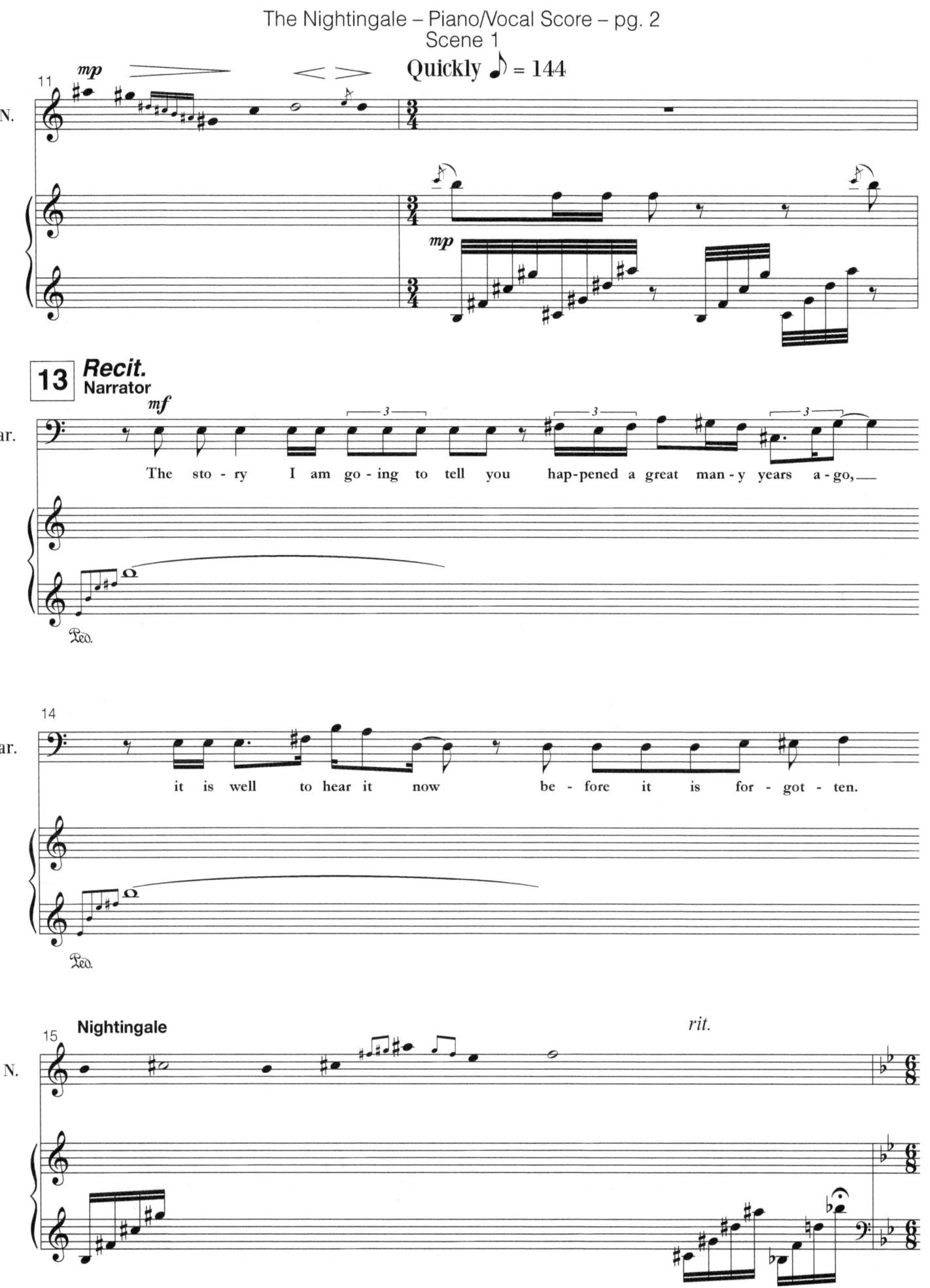

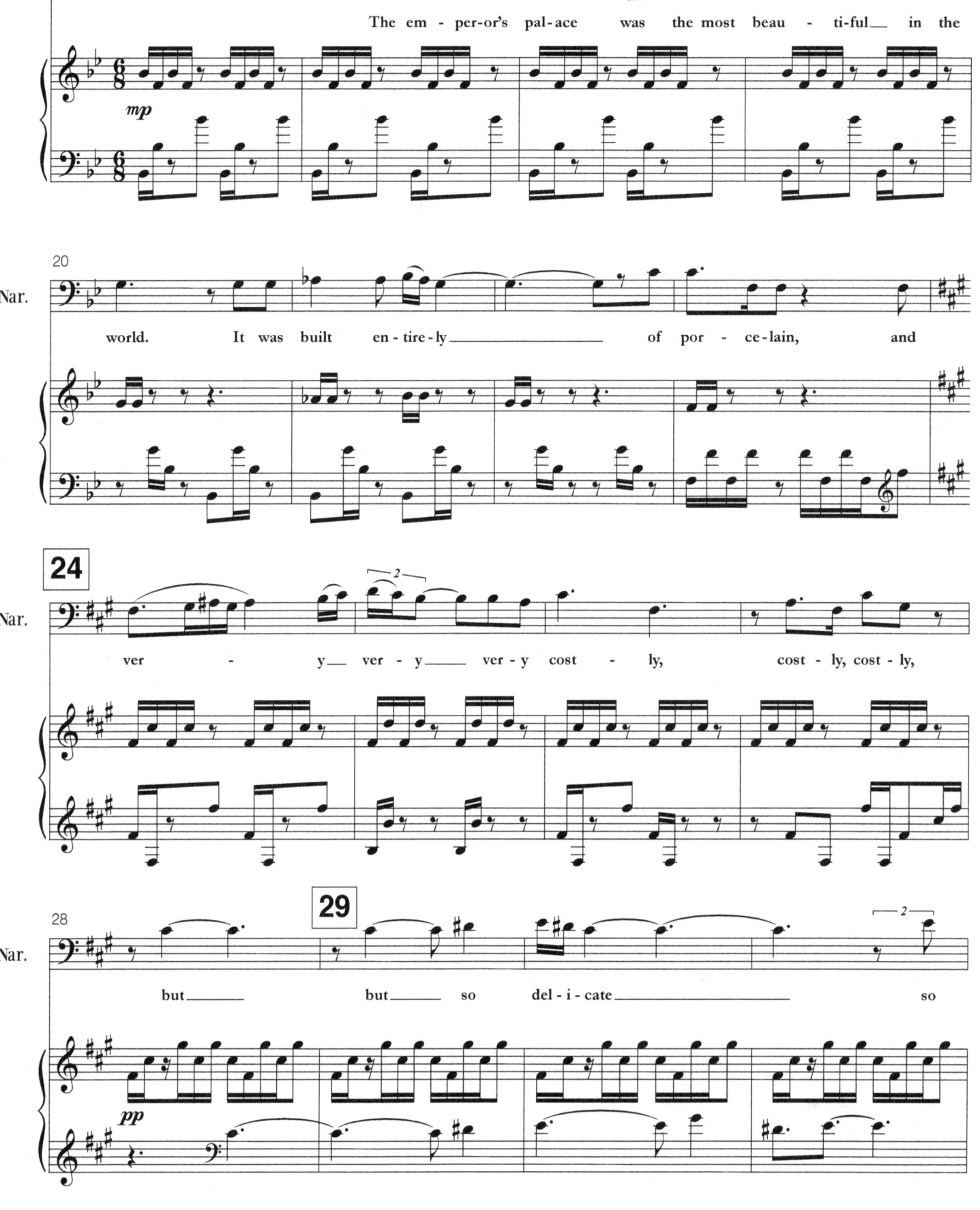

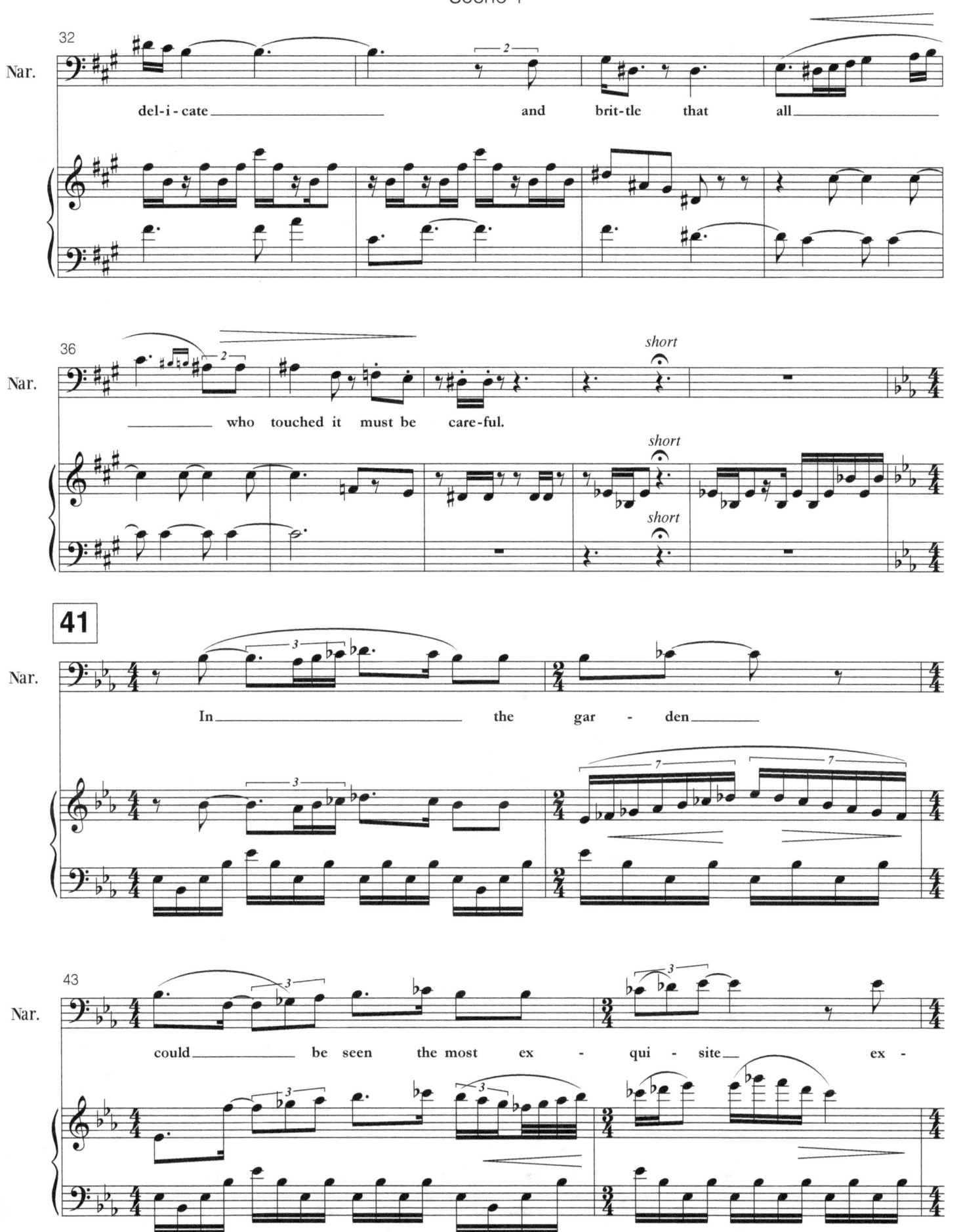

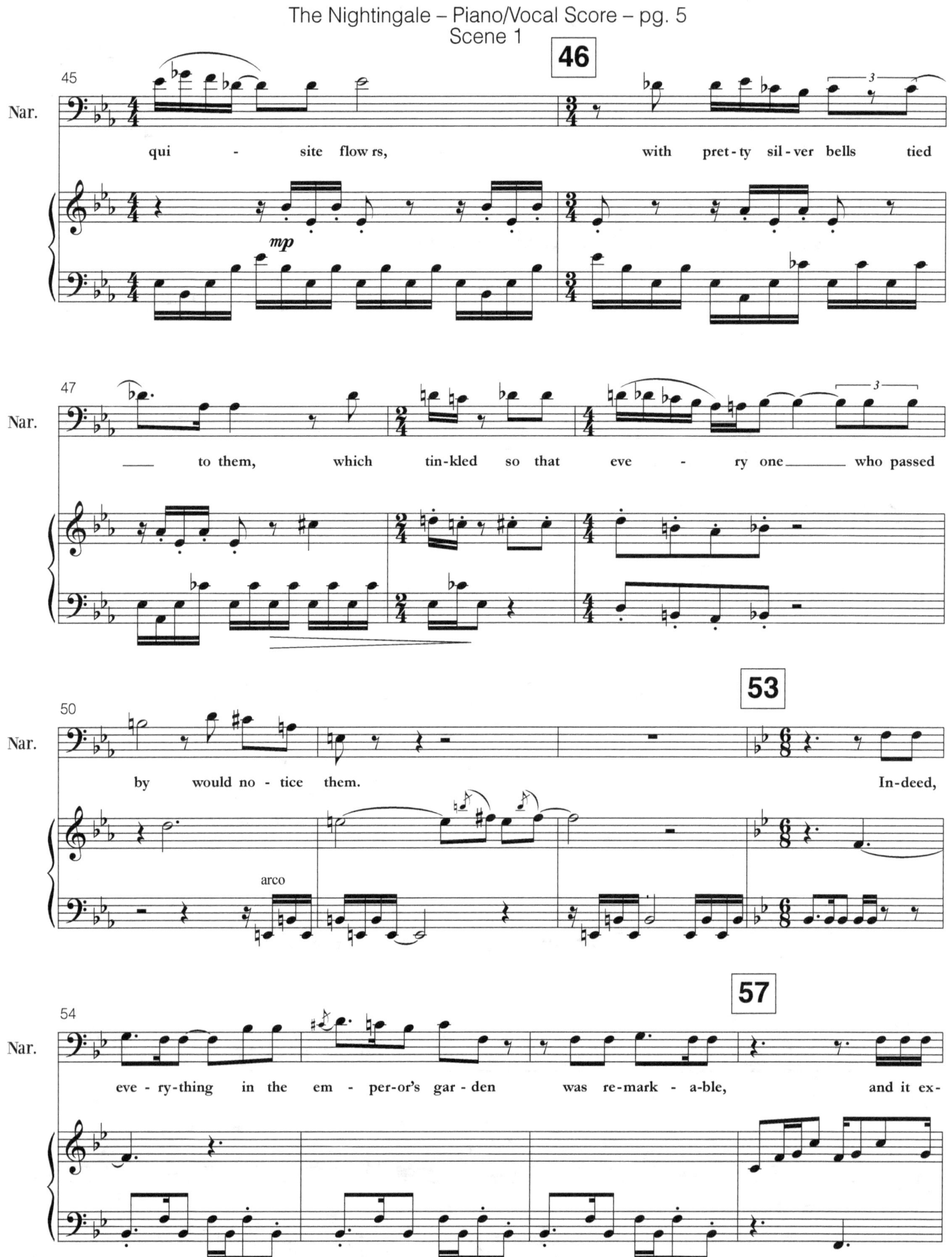

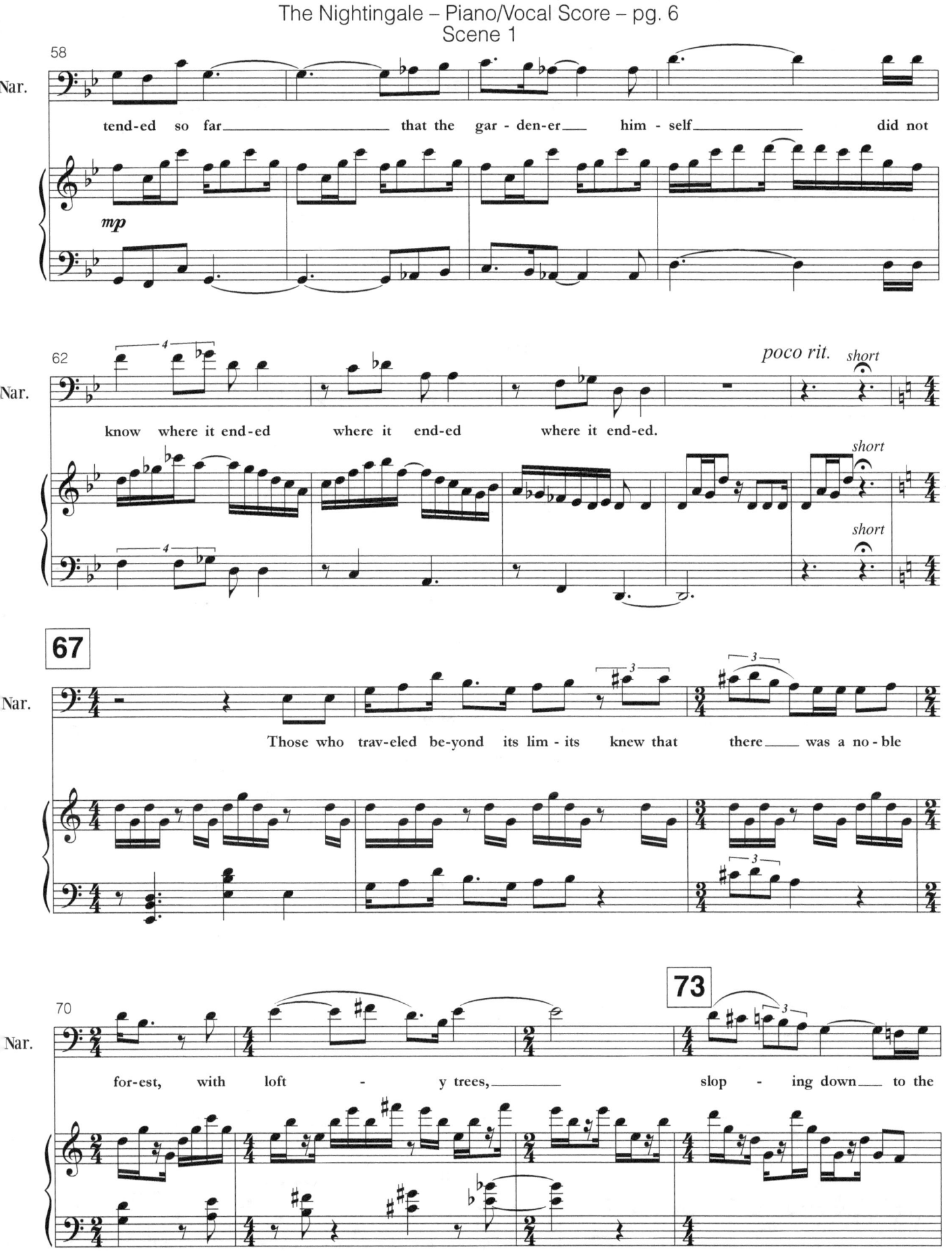

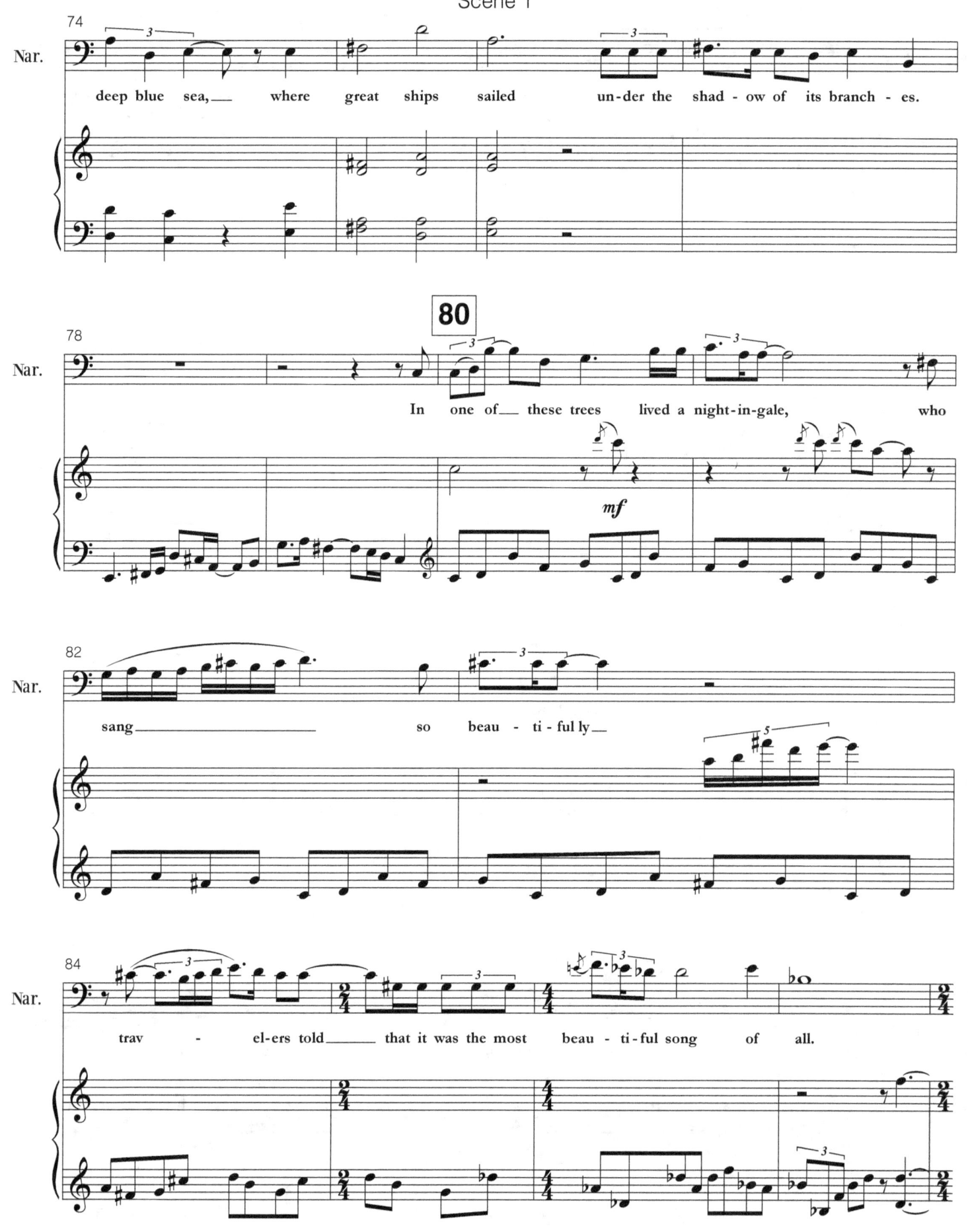

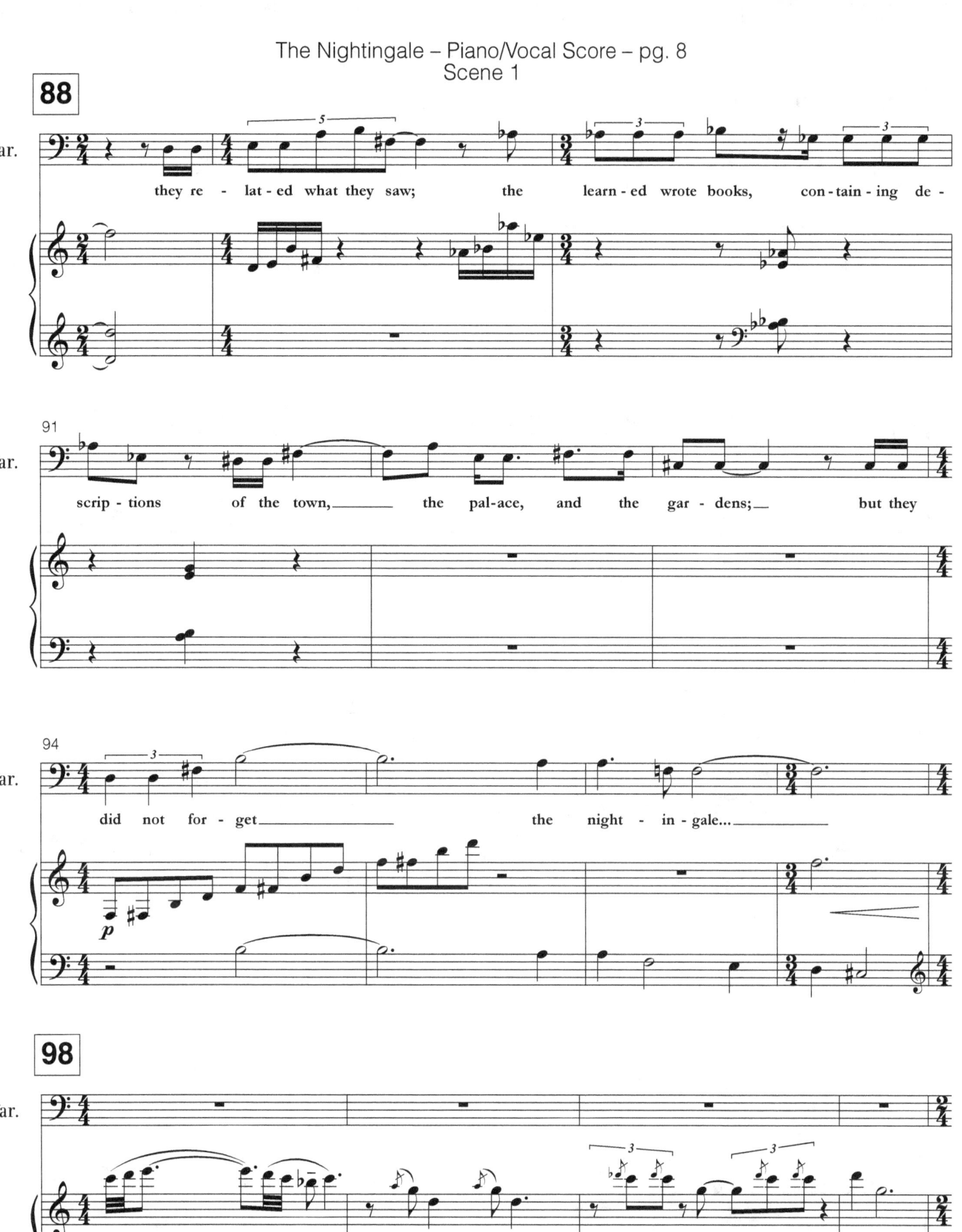

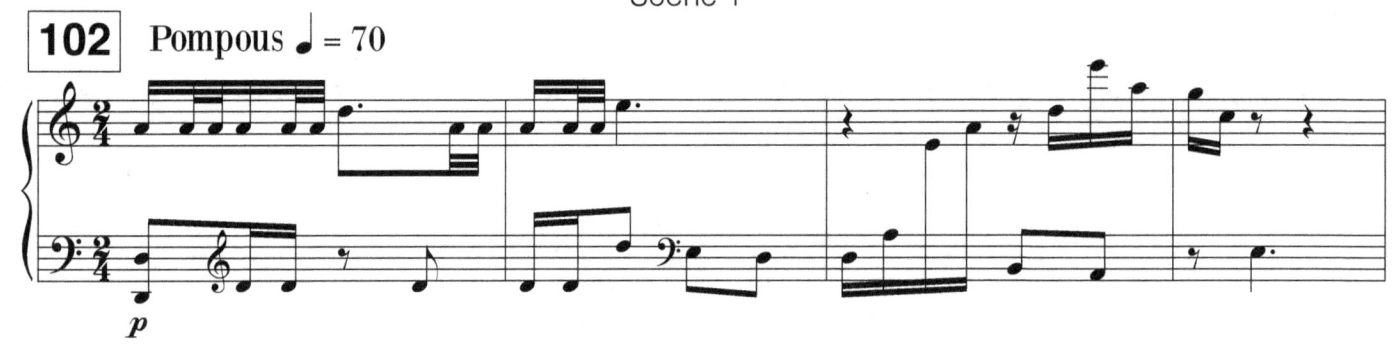

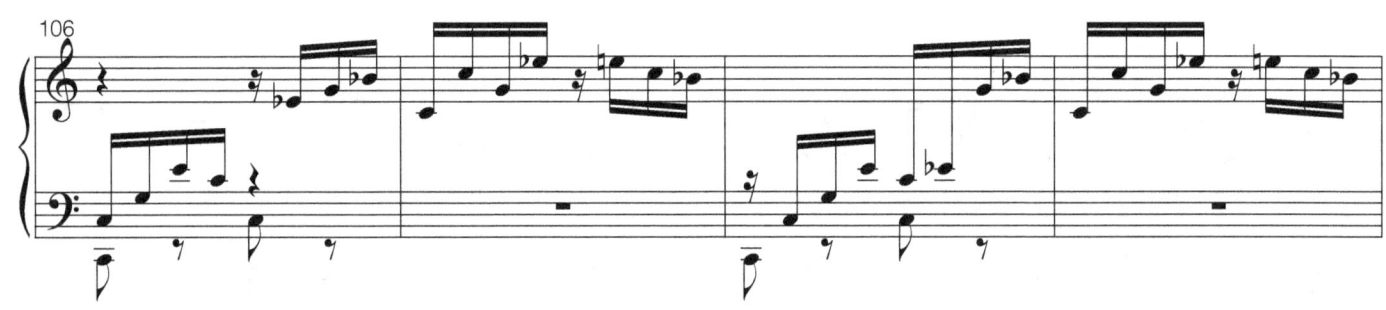

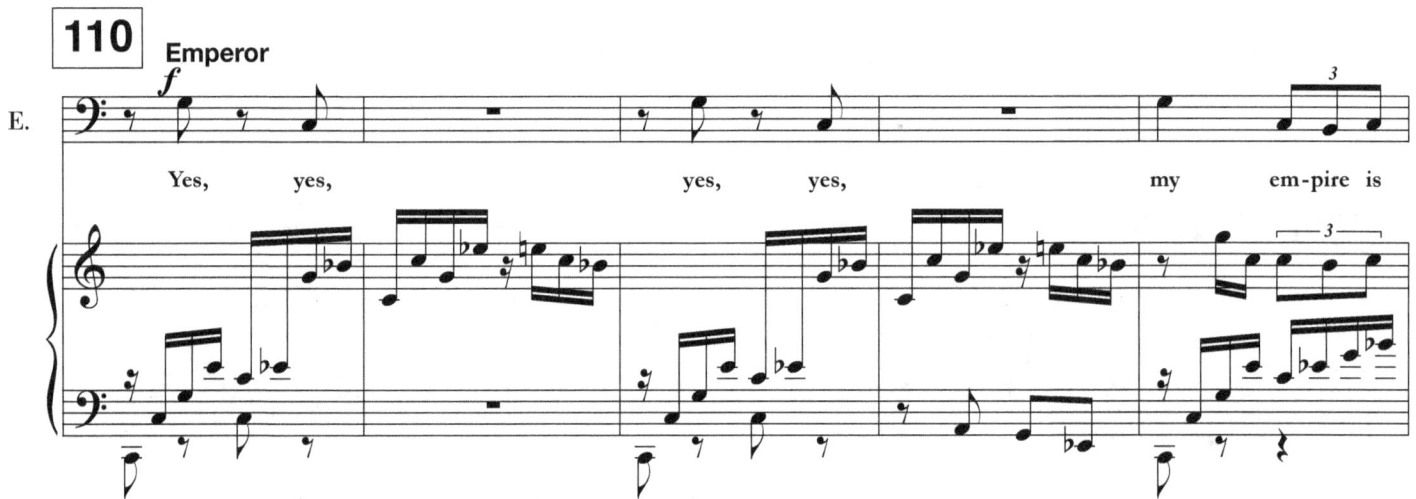

Yes,   yes,   yes,   yes,   my em-pire is

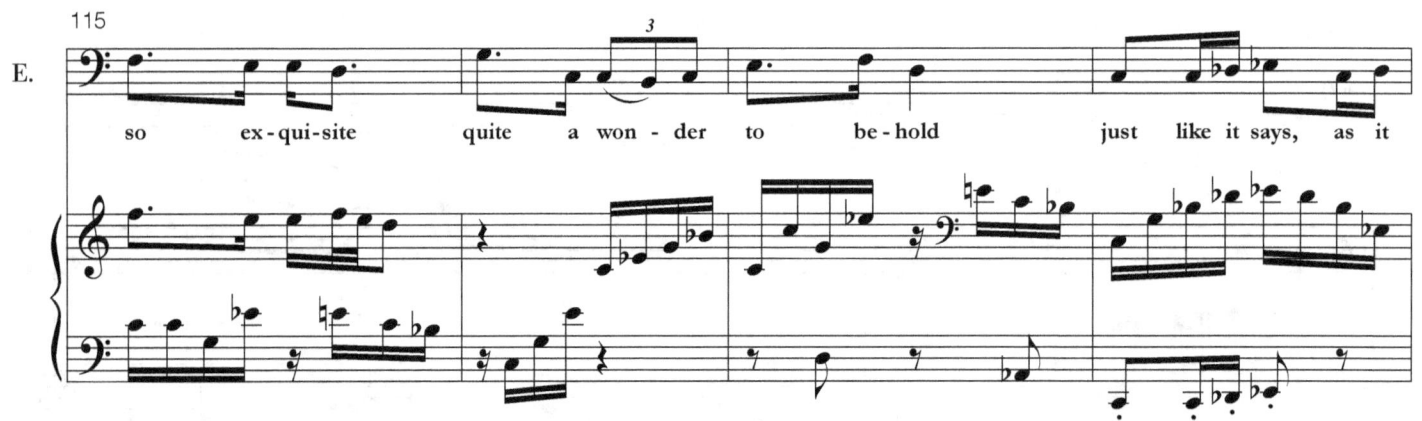

so ex-qui-site   quite a won-der to be-hold   just like it says, as it

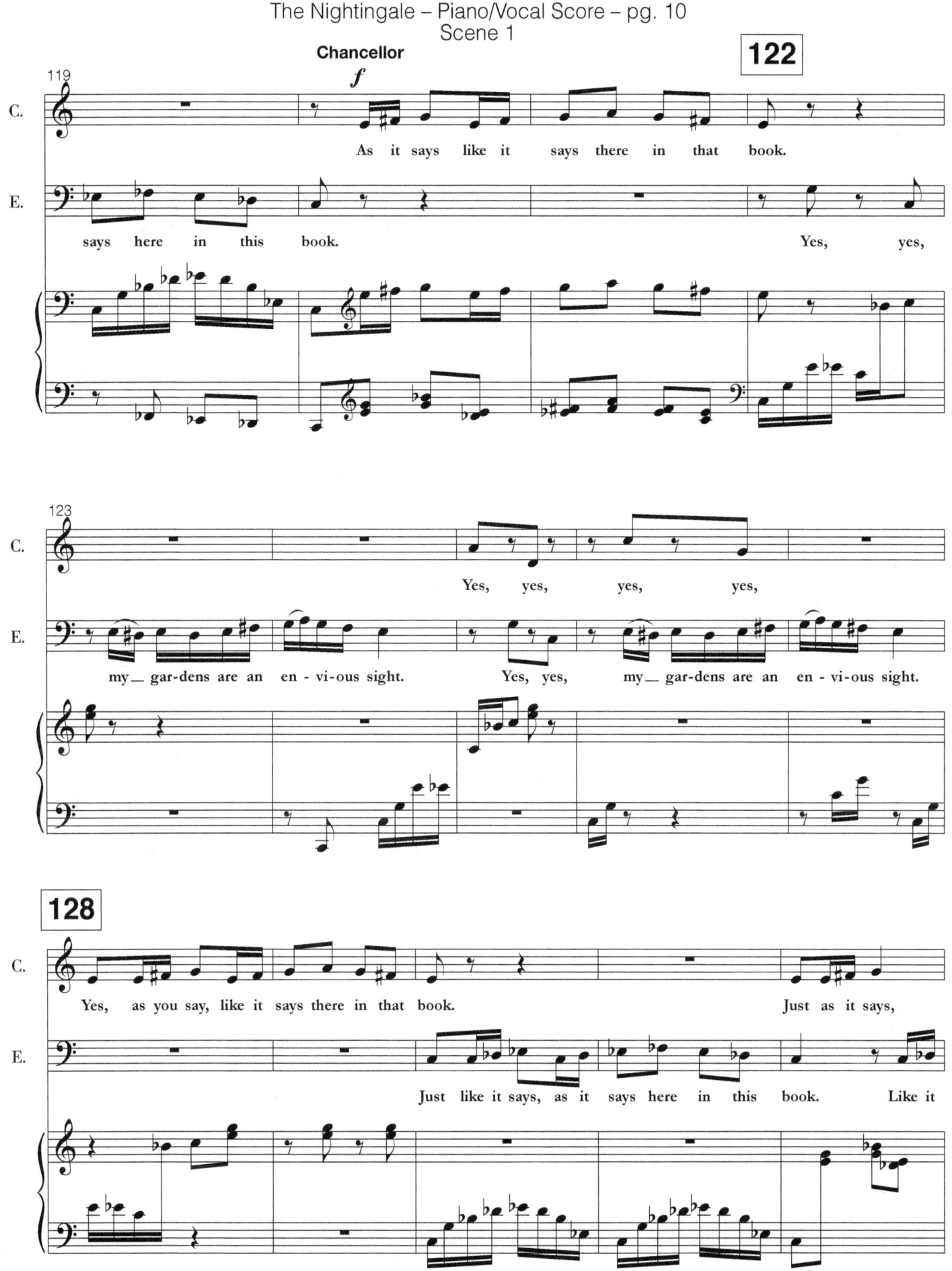

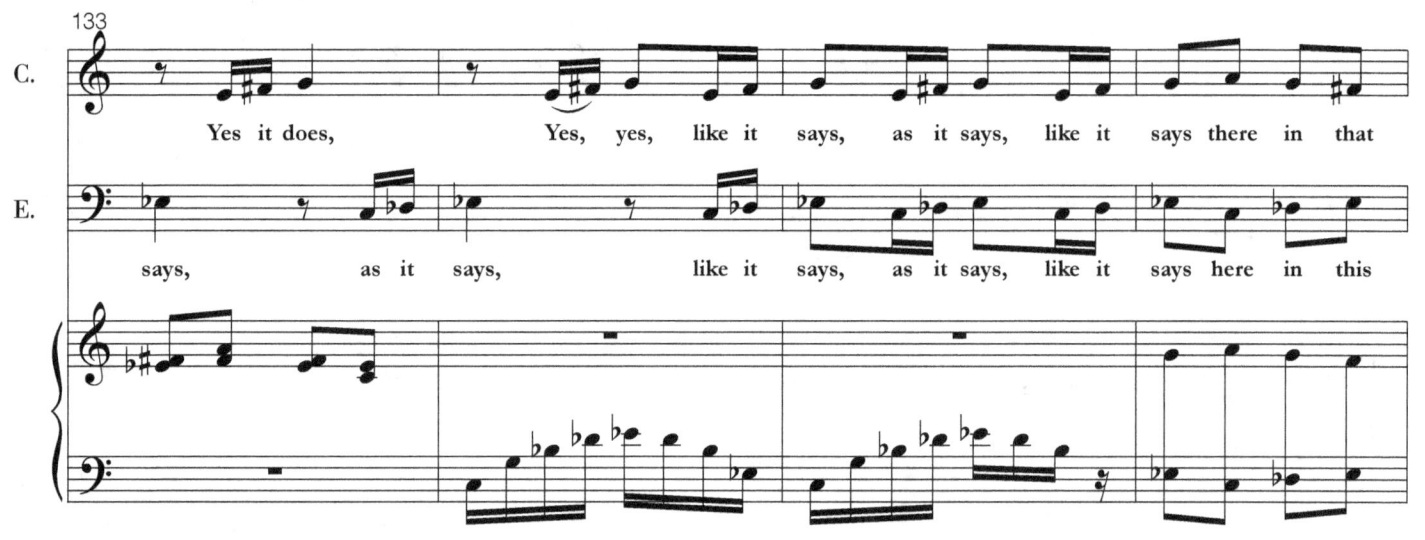

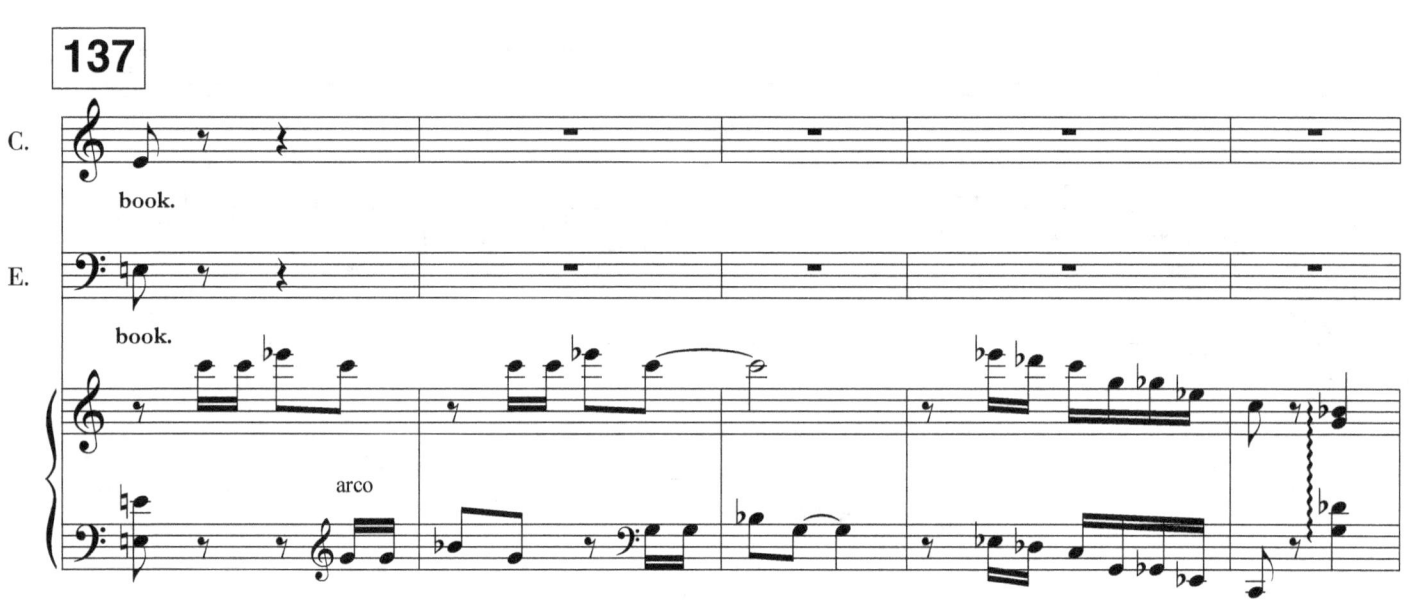

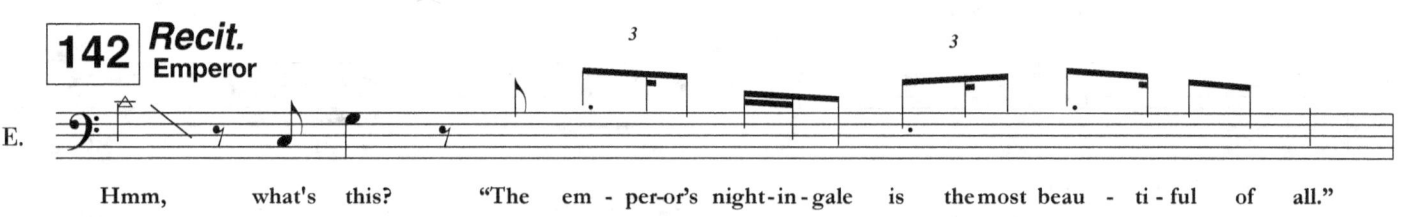

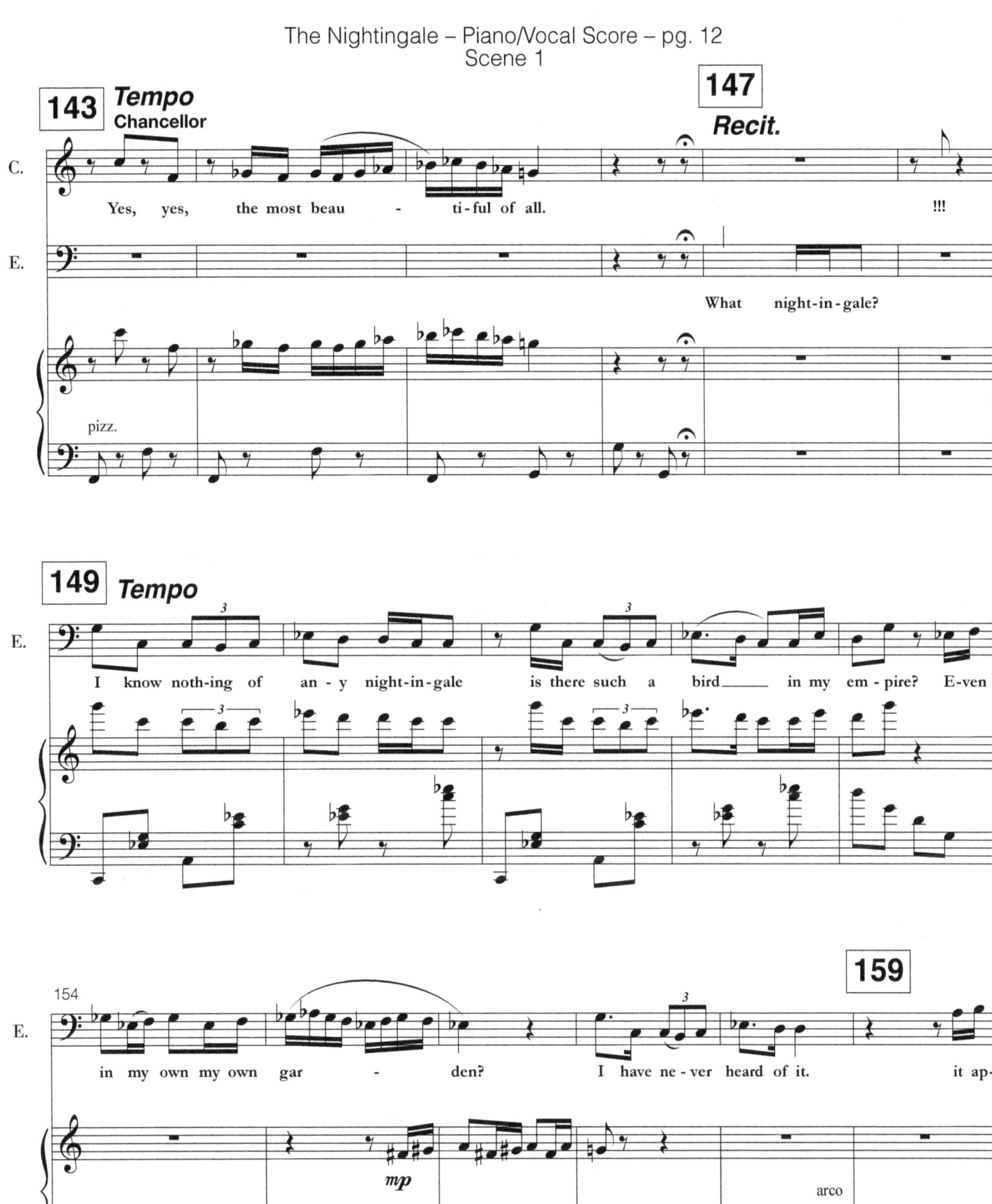

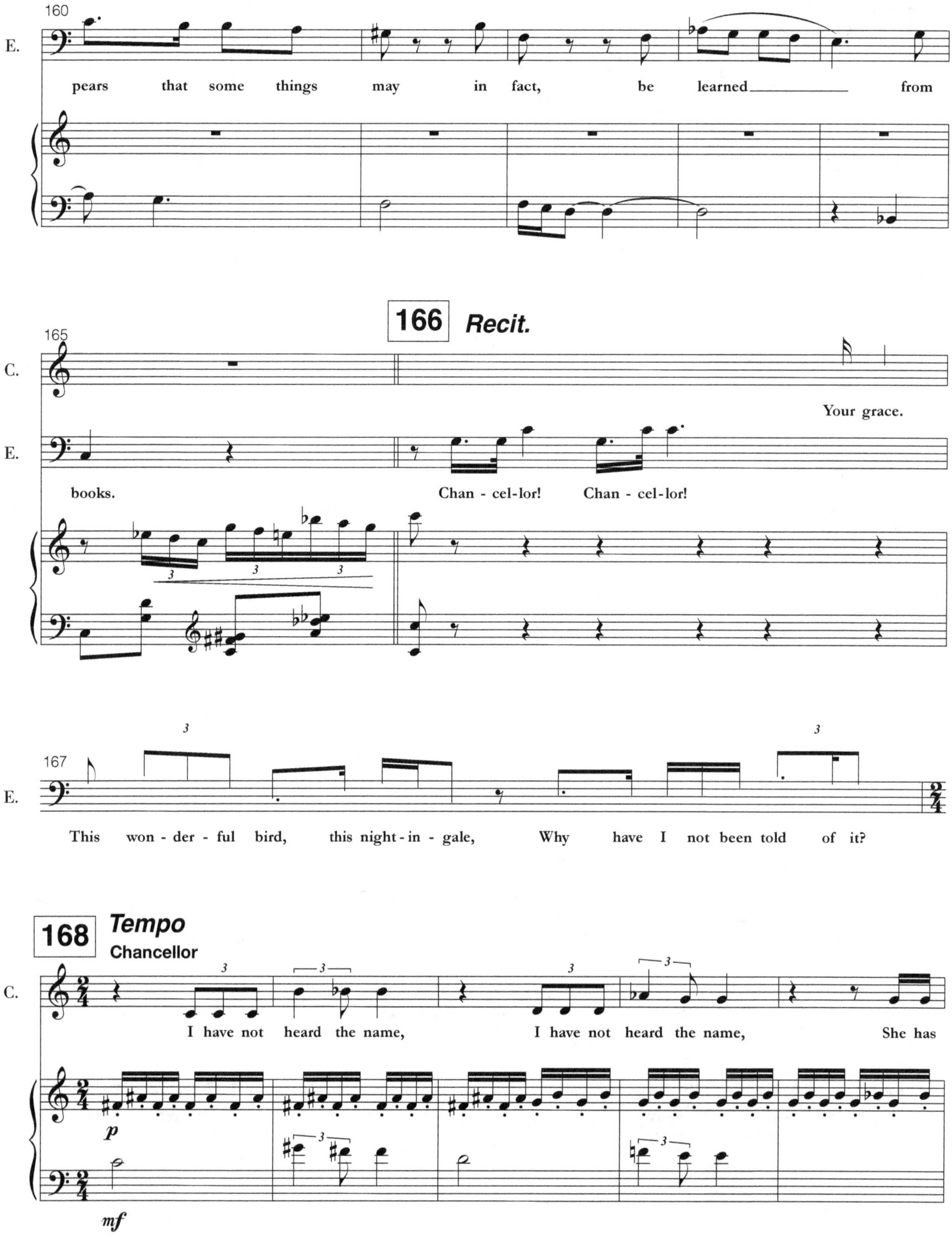

160

E.

pears that some things may in fact, be learned_____ from

166 *Recit.*

165

C.

Your grace.

E.

books. Chan - cel-lor! Chan - cel-lor!

167

E.

This won-der-ful bird, this night-in-gale, Why have I not been told of it?

168 *Tempo*
Chancellor

C.

I have not heard the name, I have not heard the name, She has

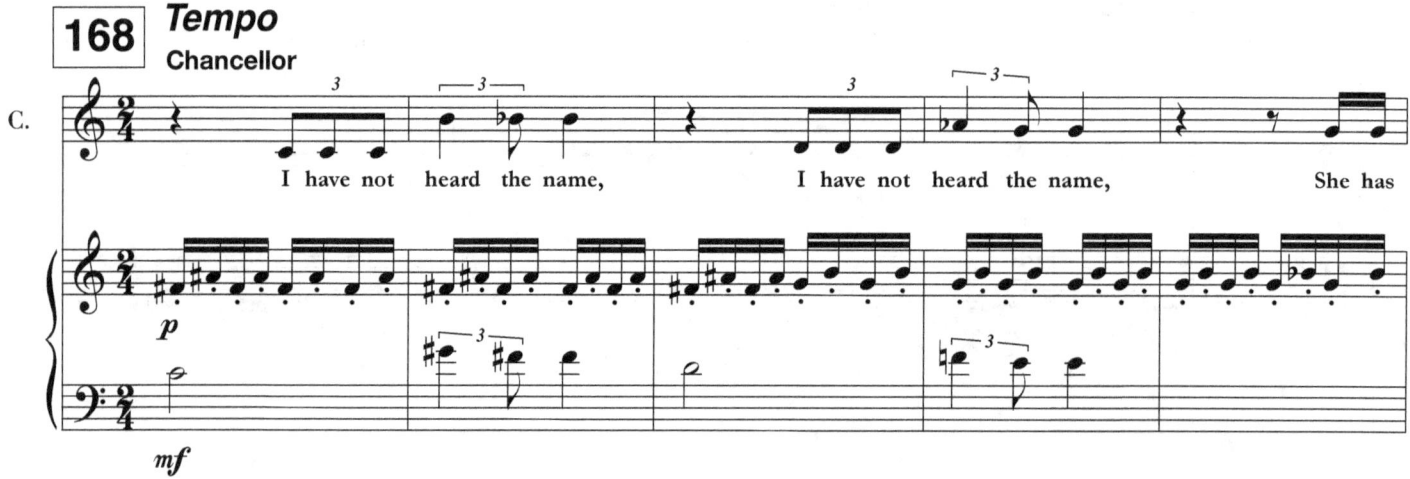

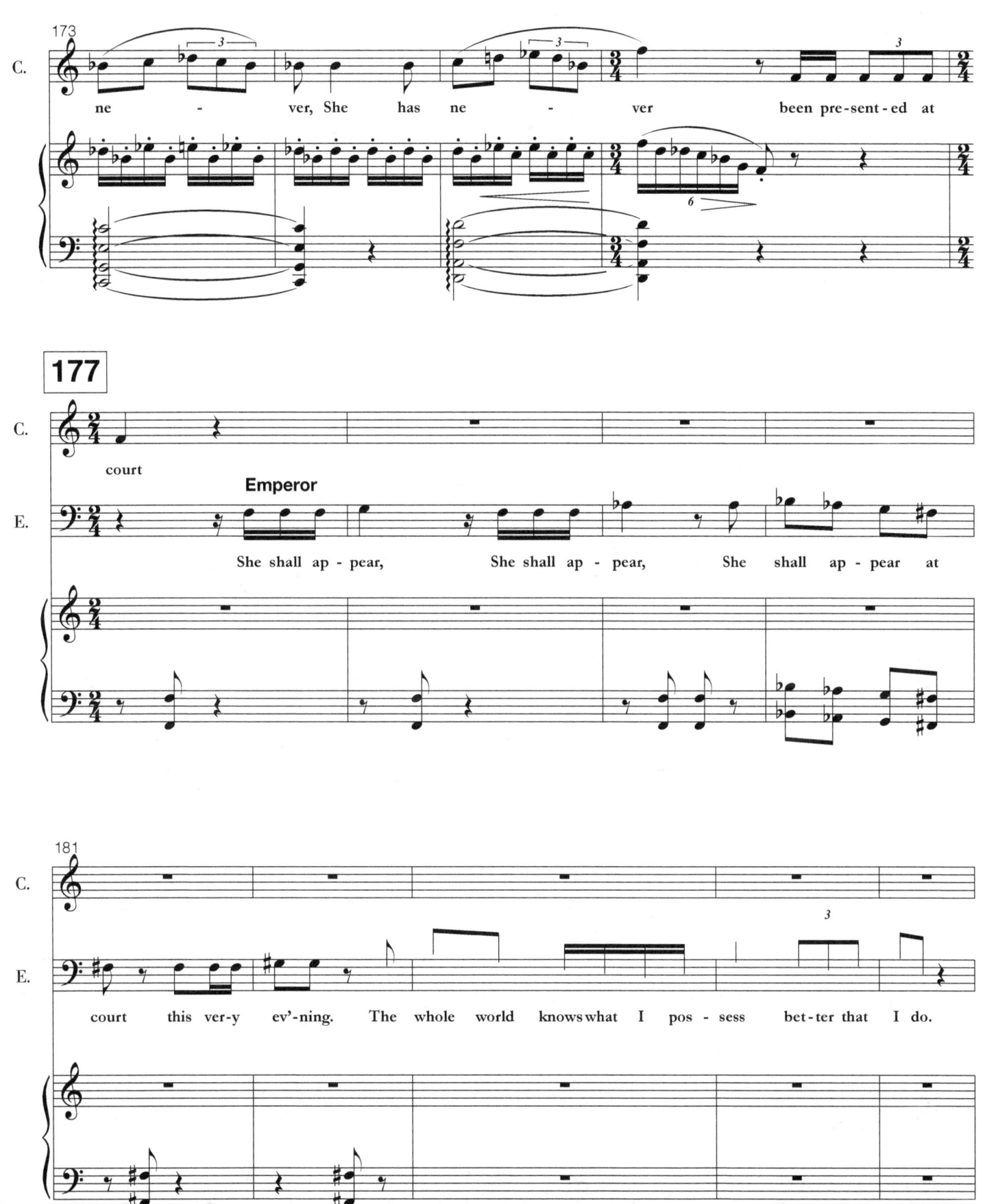

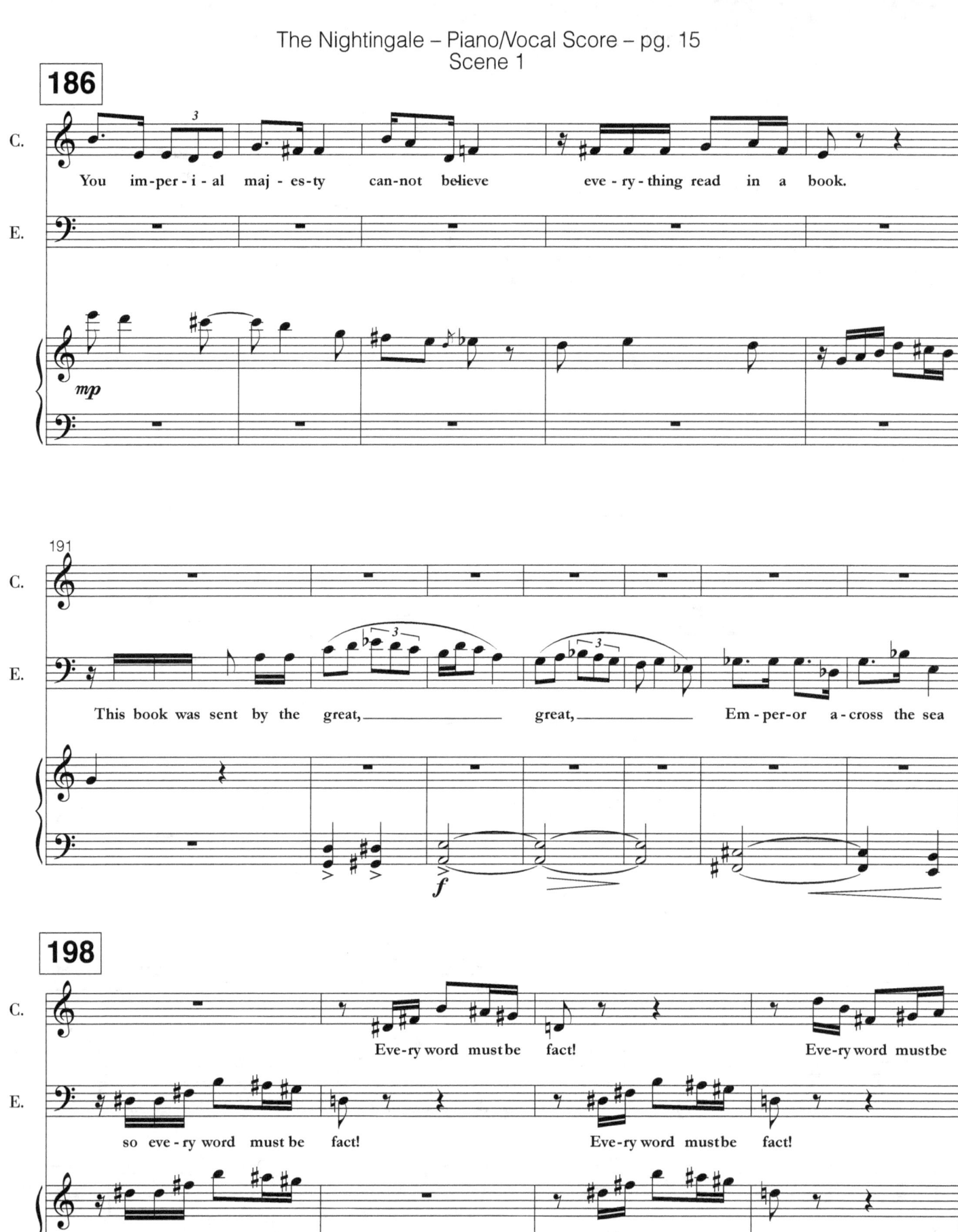

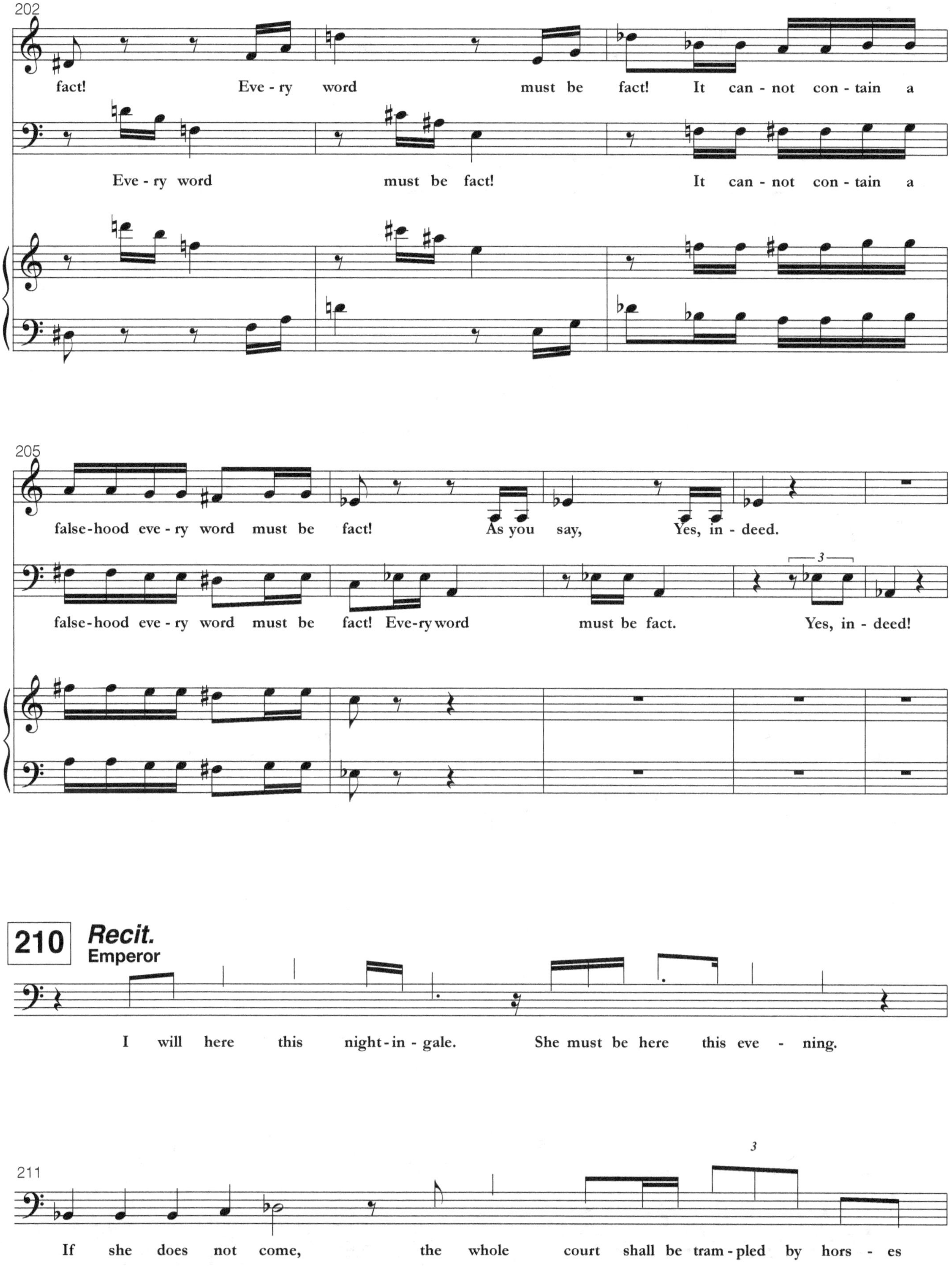

202

C. fact! Eve - ry word must be fact! It can - not con - tain a

E. Eve - ry word must be fact! It can - not con - tain a

205

C. false-hood eve - ry word must be fact! As you say, Yes, in - deed.

E. false-hood eve - ry word must be fact! Eve - ry word must be fact. Yes, in - deed!

210 *Recit.*
Emperor

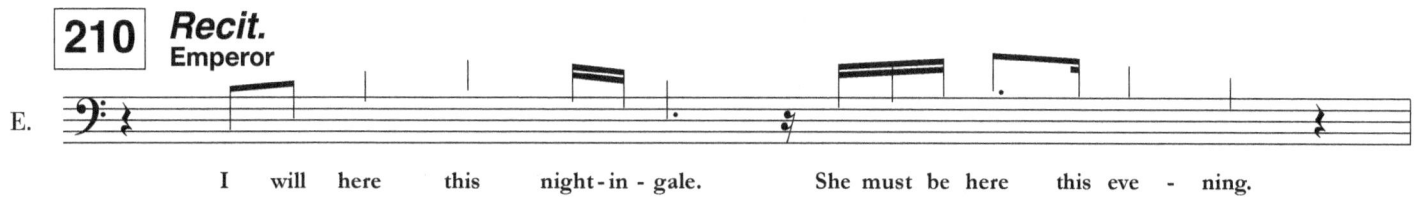

E. I will here this night-in-gale. She must be here this eve - ning.

211

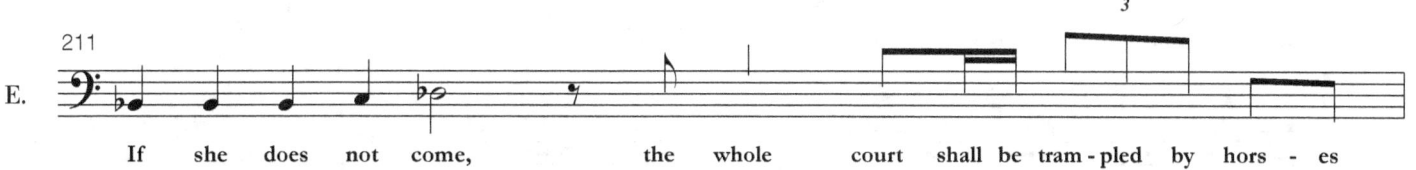

E. If she does not come, the whole court shall be tram-pled by hors - es

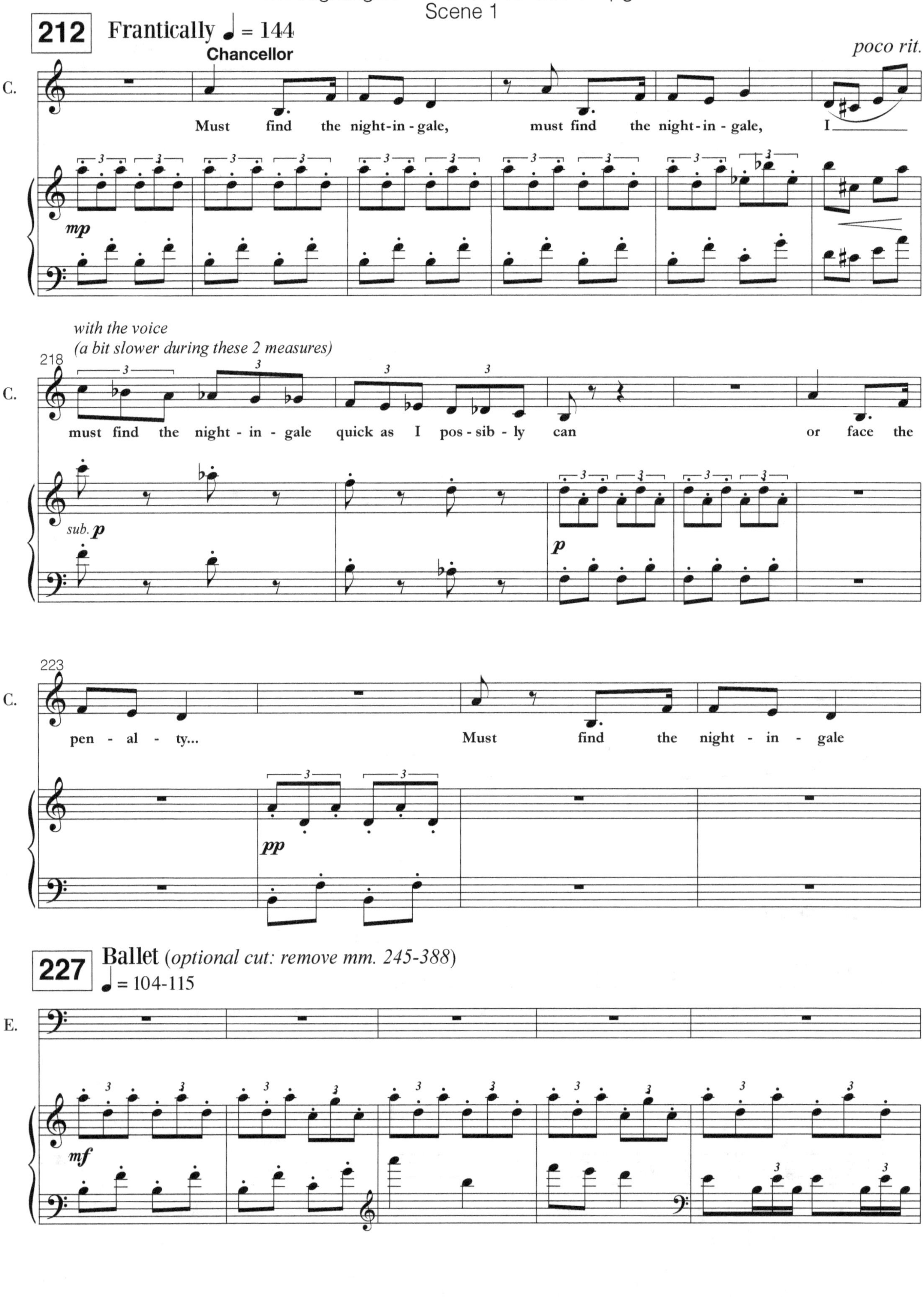

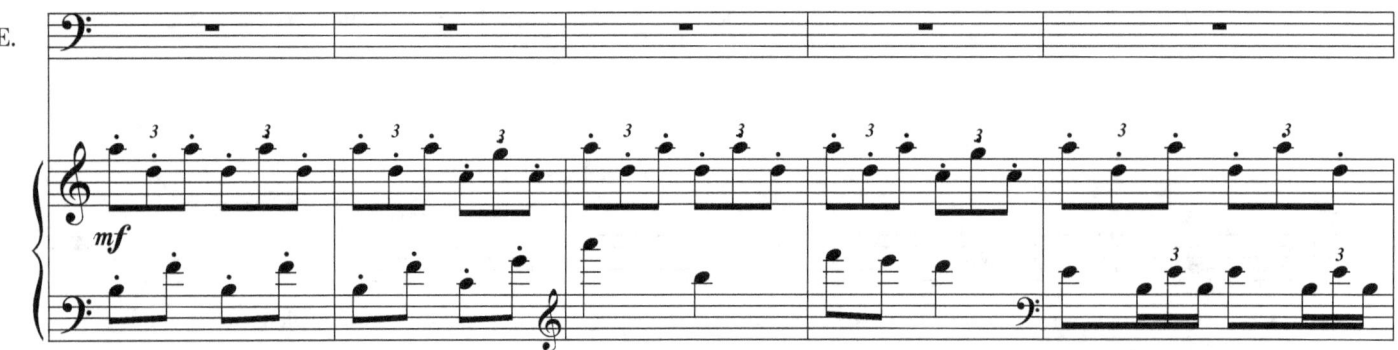

212 **Frantically** ♩ = 144

Chancellor

poco rit.

C.

Must find the night-in-gale, must find the night-in-gale, I

mp

with the voice
(a bit slower during these 2 measures)

218

C.

must find the night-in-gale quick as I pos-sib-ly can or face the

sub. *p*

p

223

C.

pen - al - ty... Must find the night - in - gale

pp

227 **Ballet** *(optional cut: remove mm. 245-388)*
♩ = 104-115

E.

mf

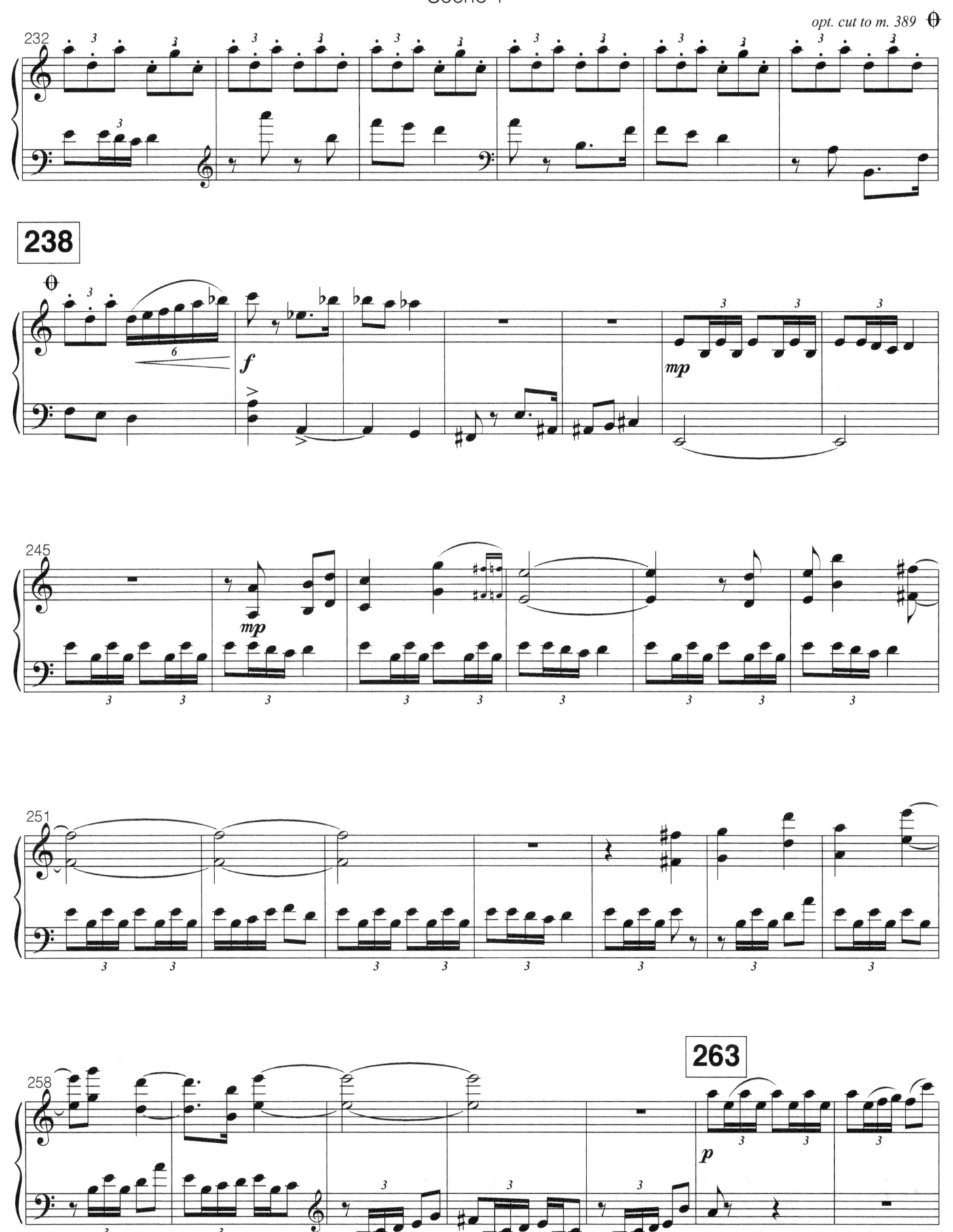

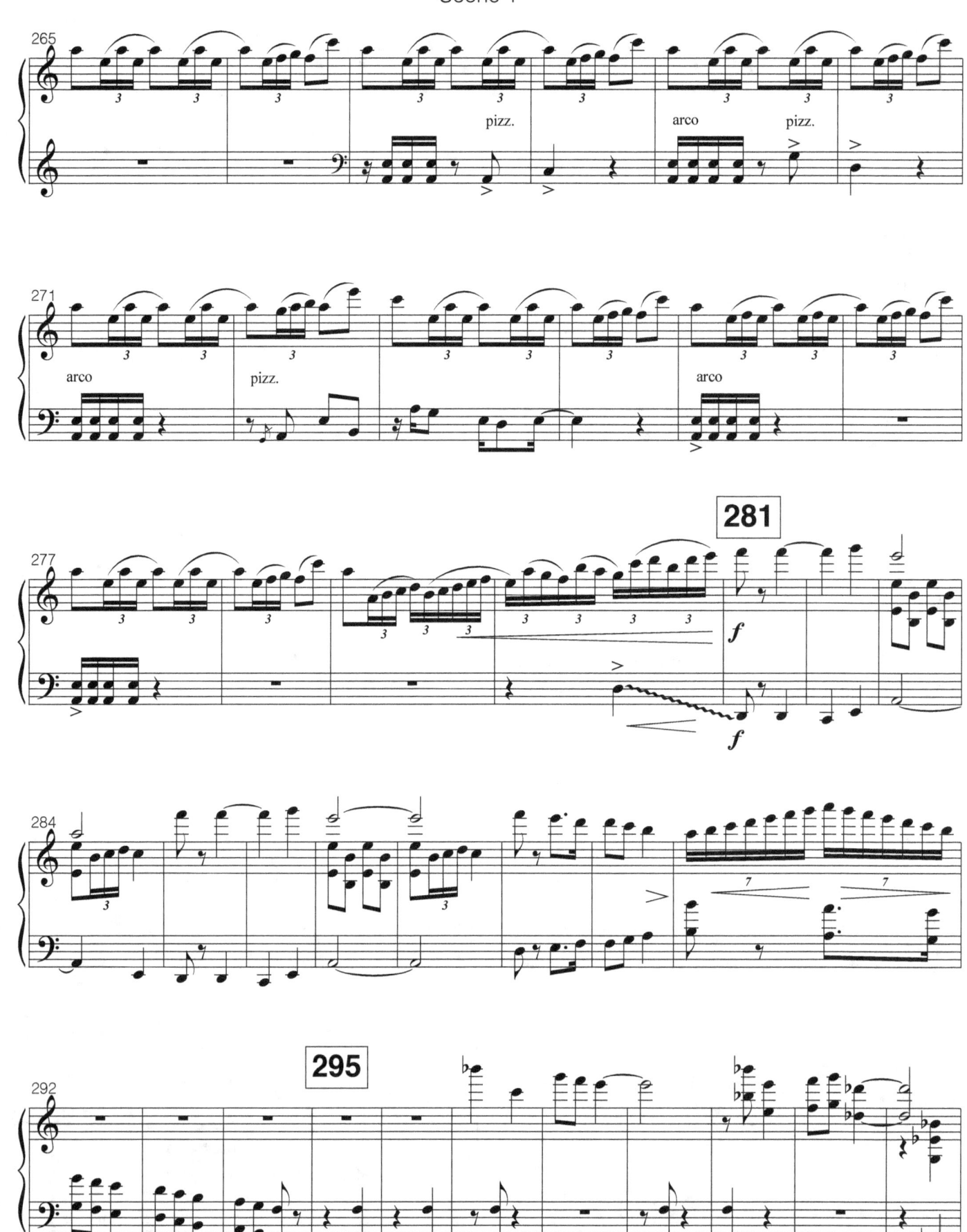

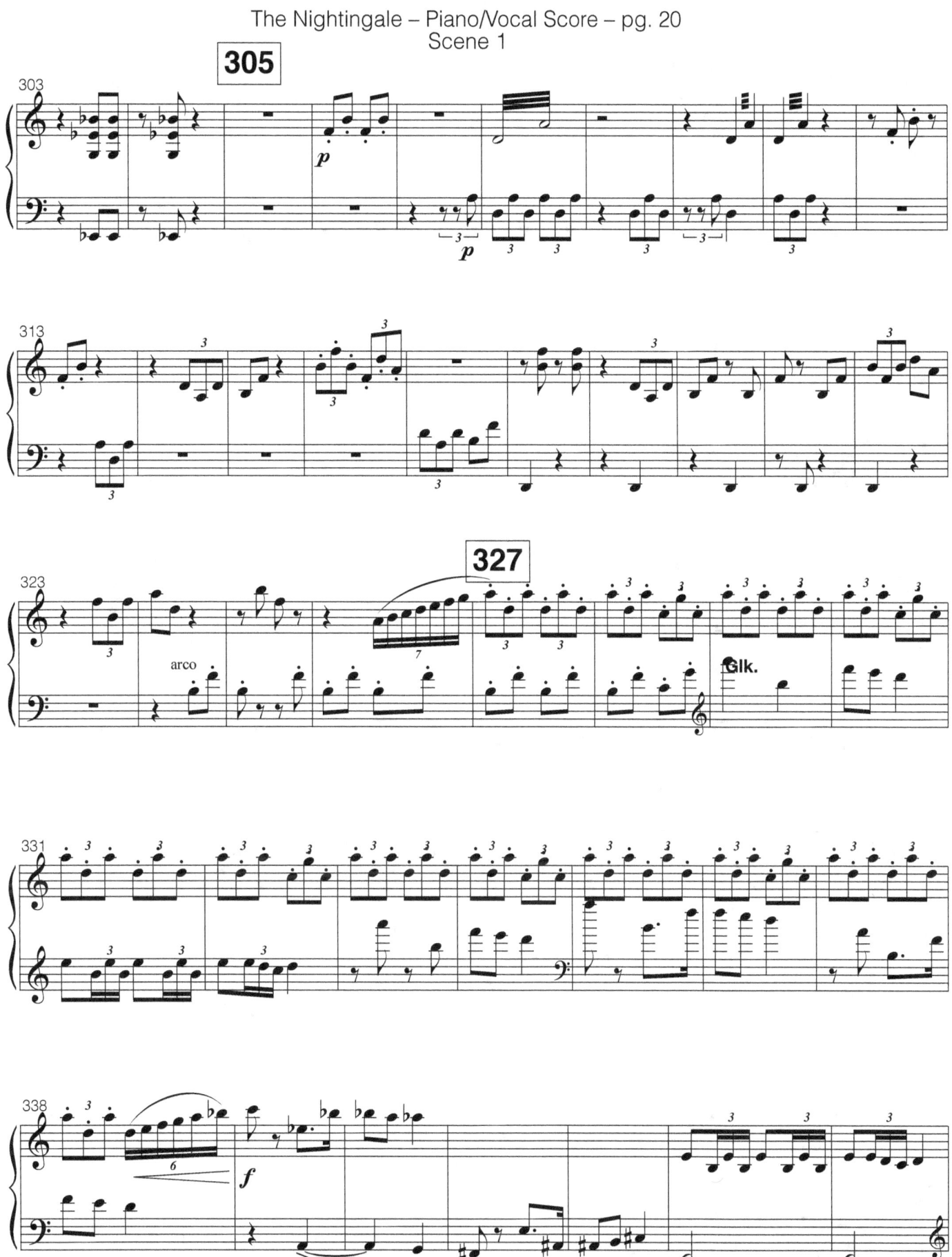

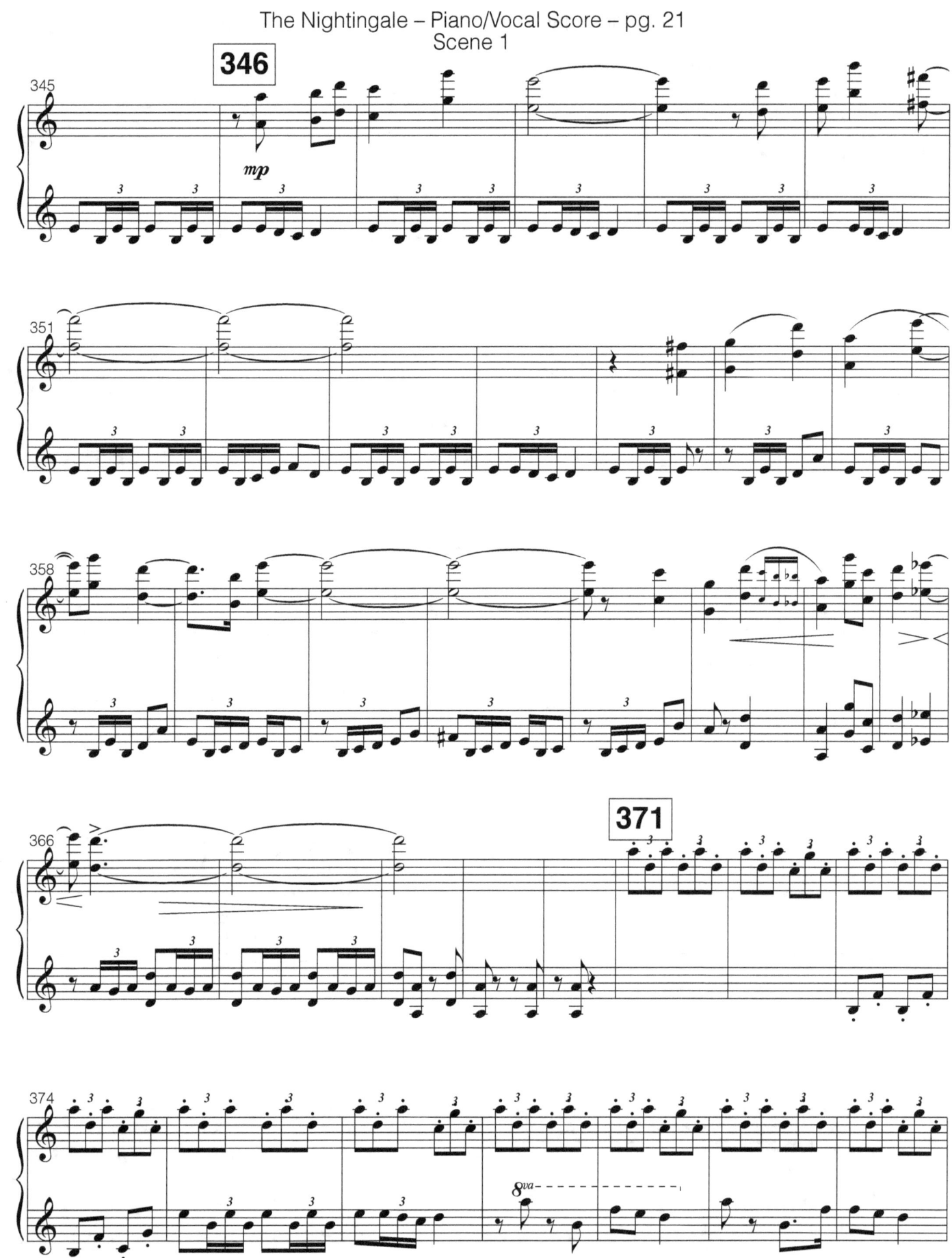

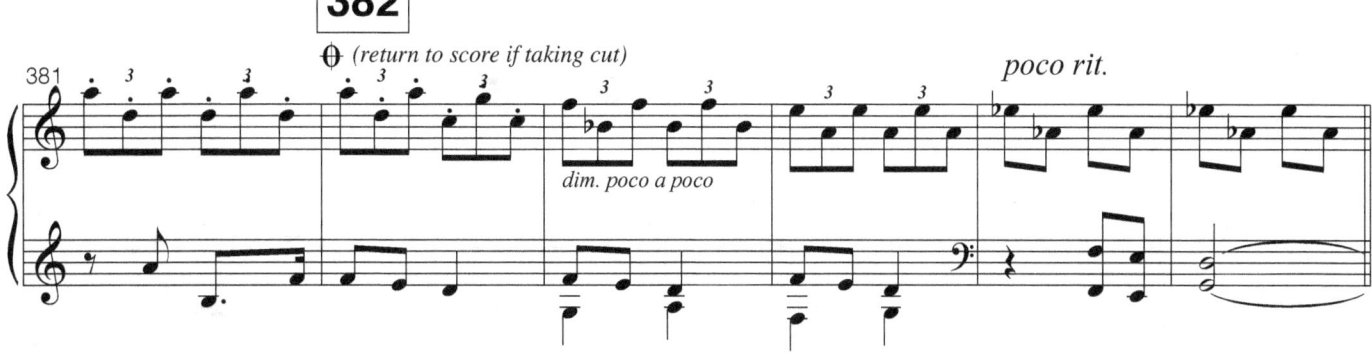

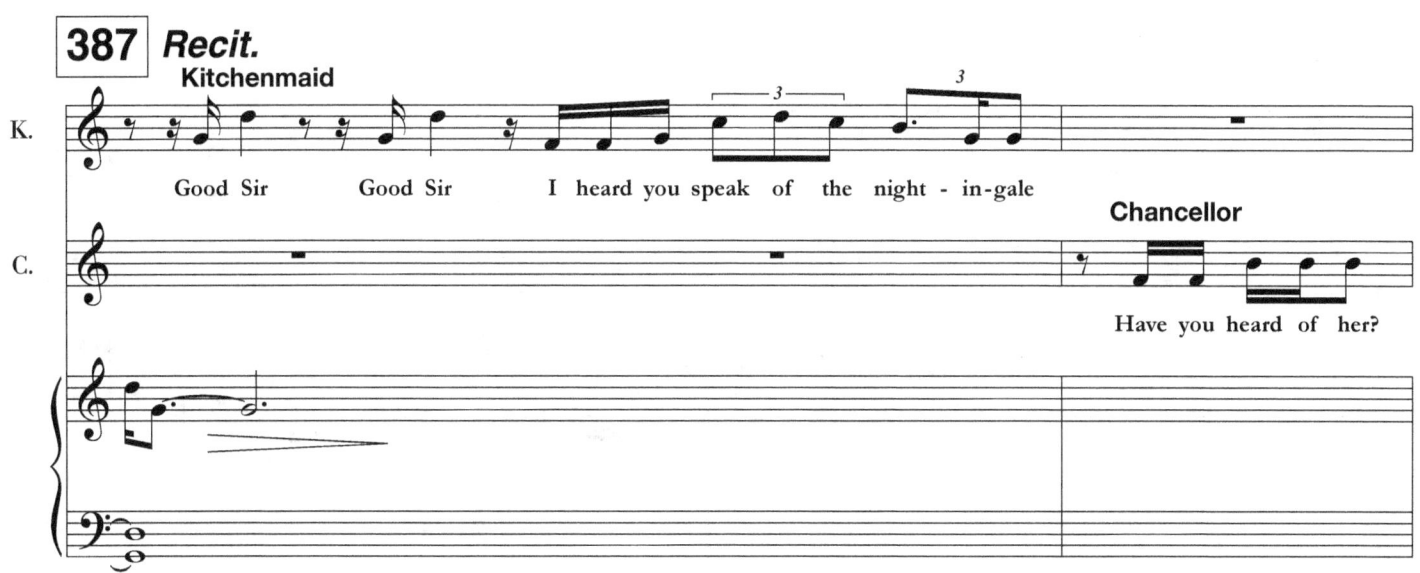

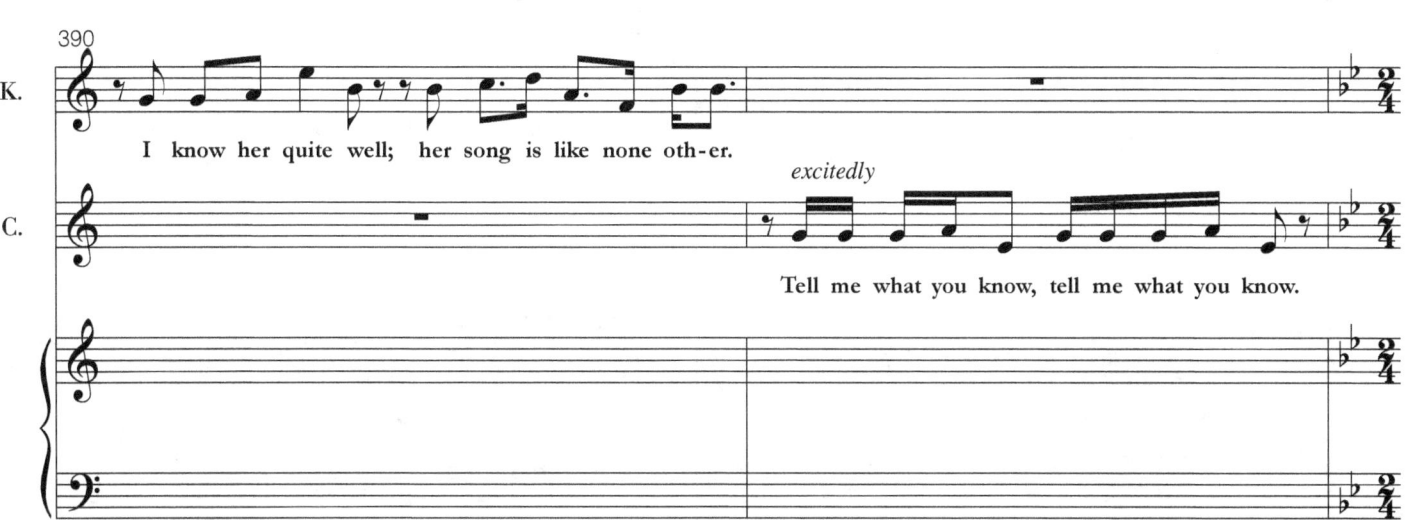

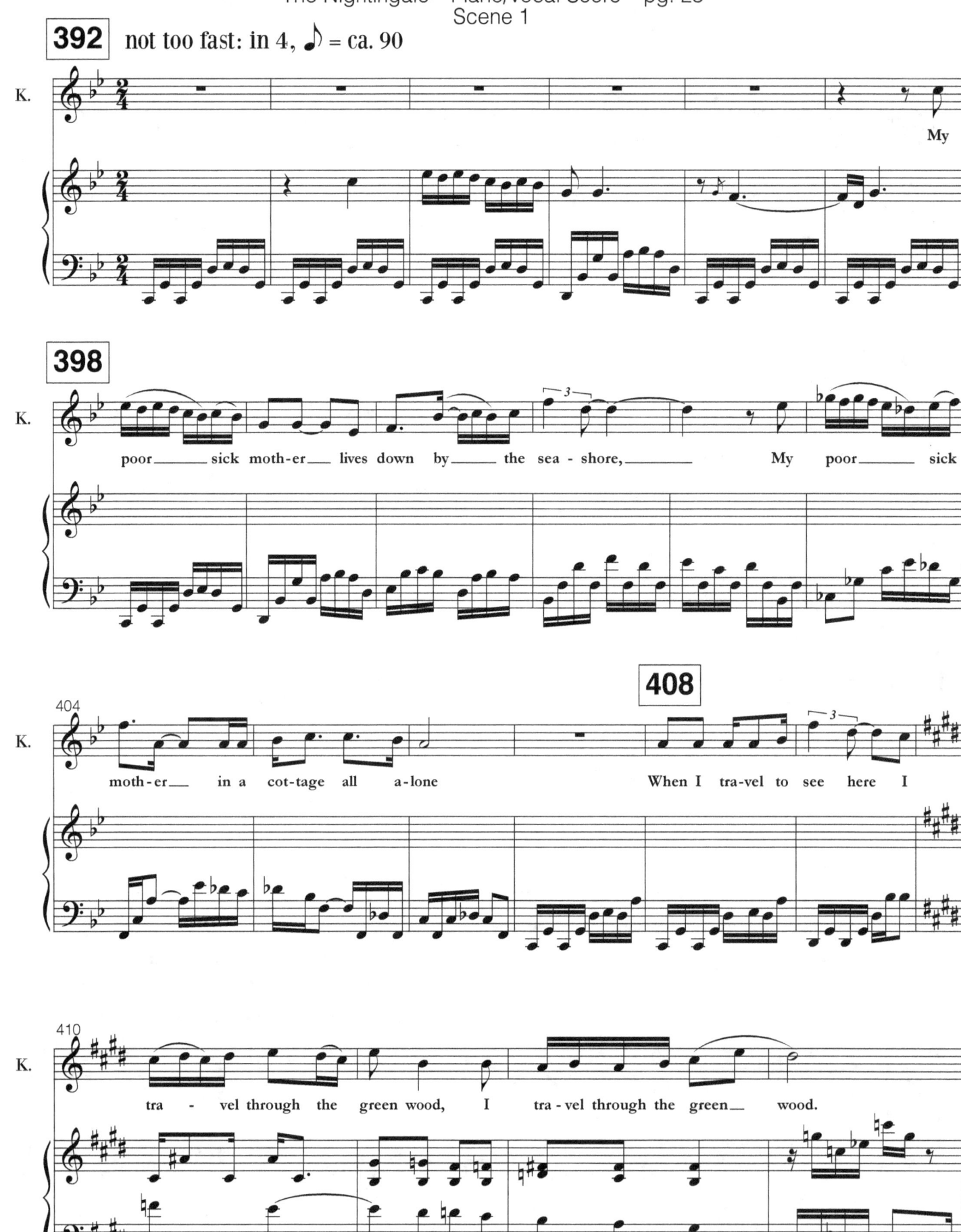

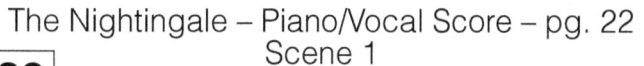

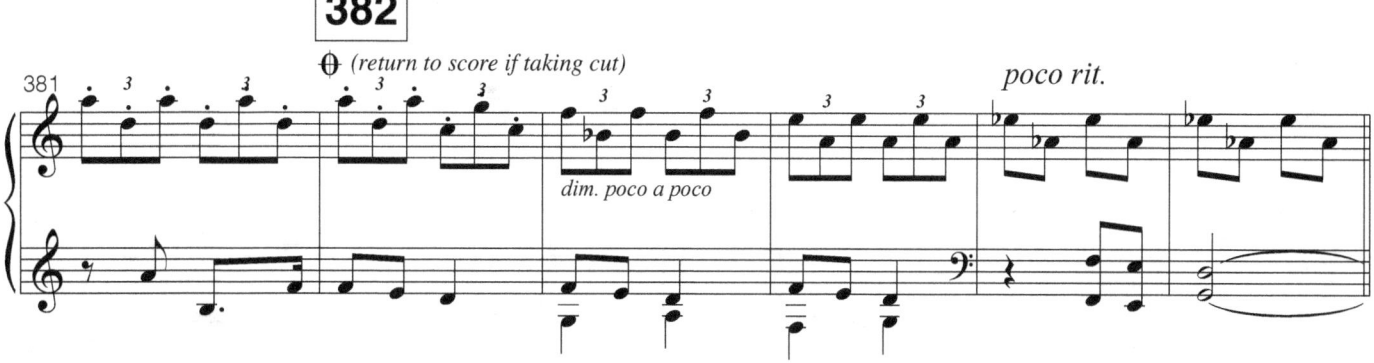

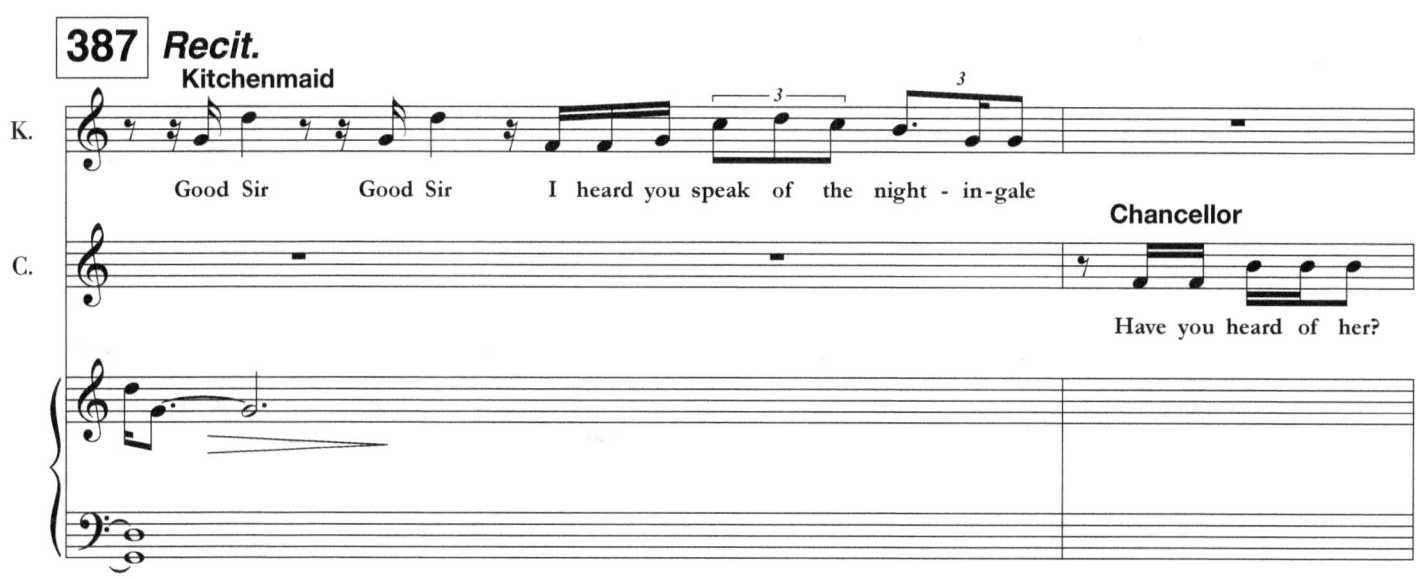

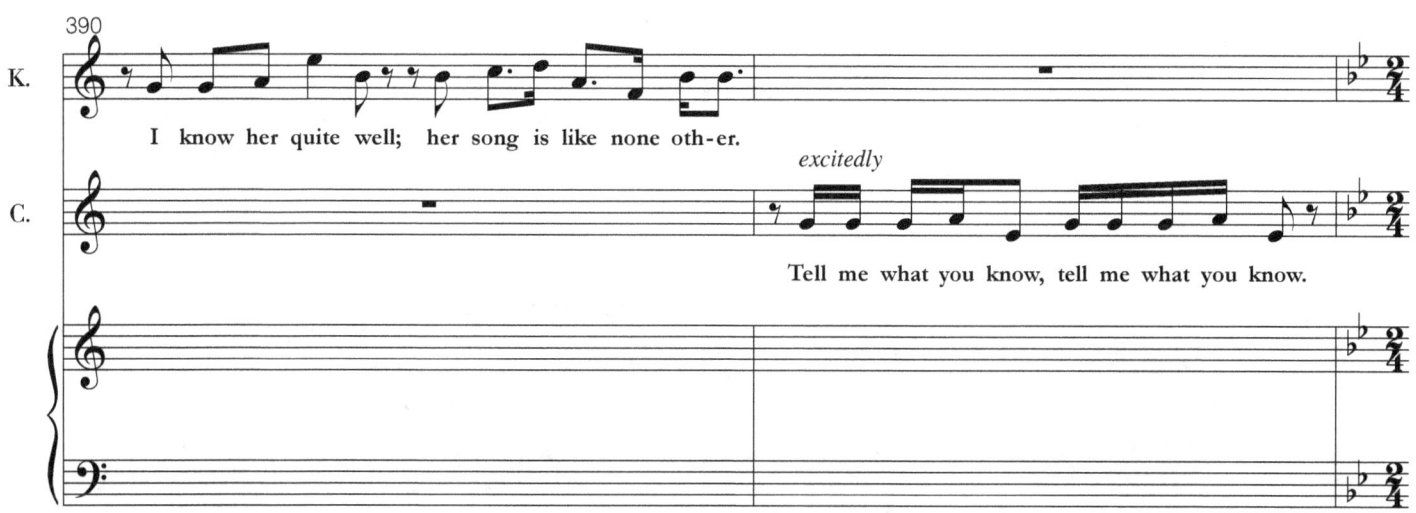

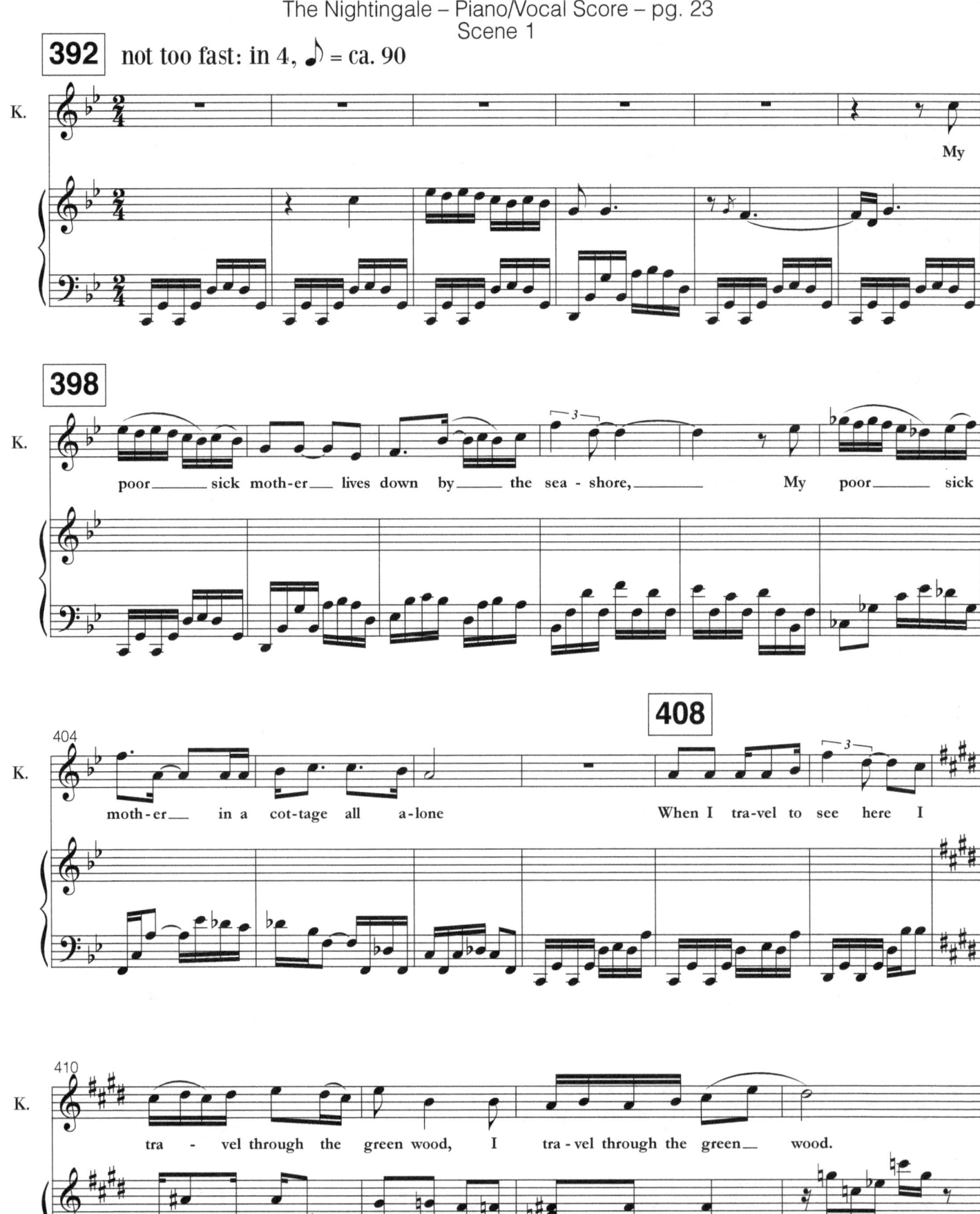

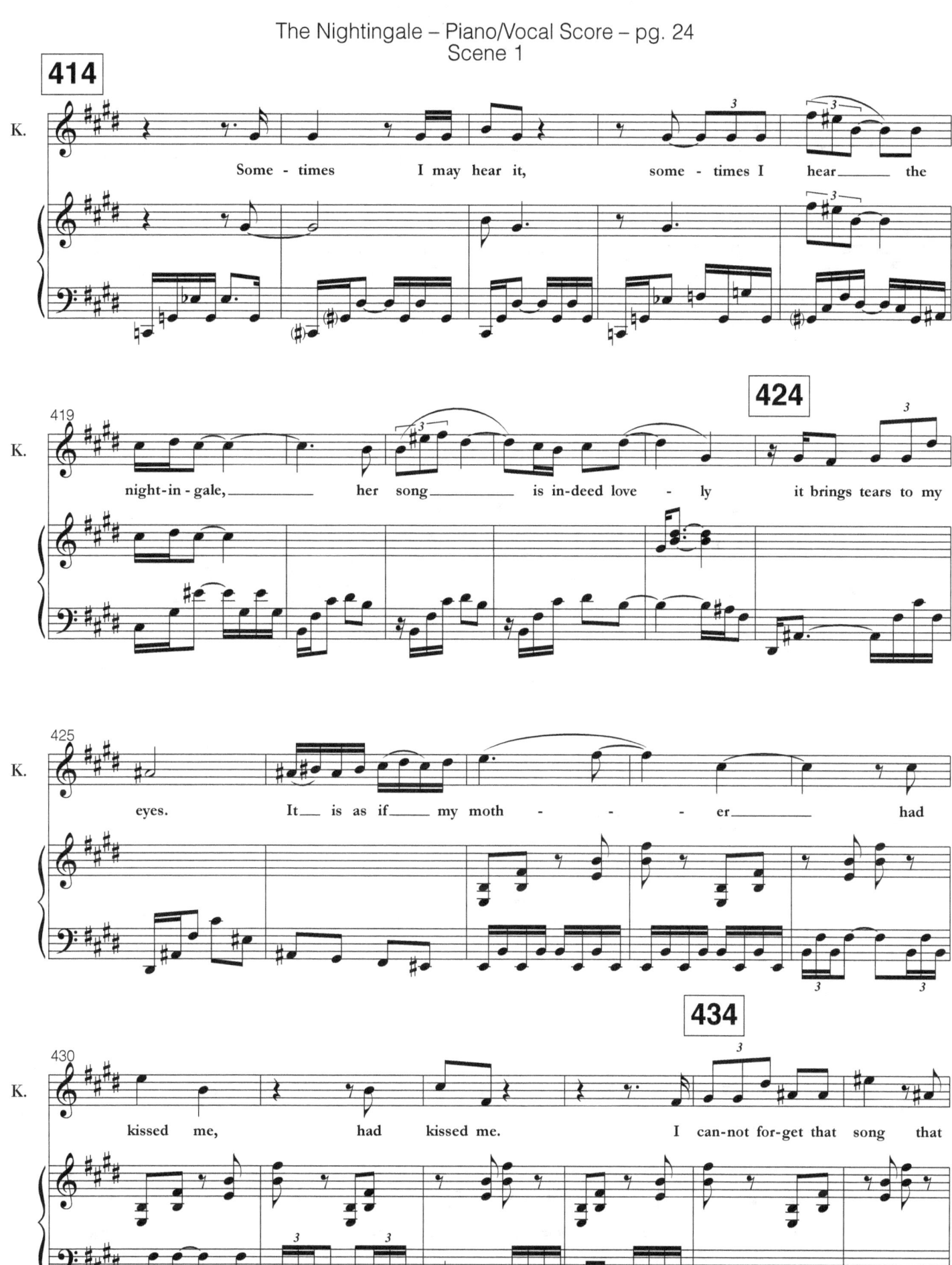

Scene 1

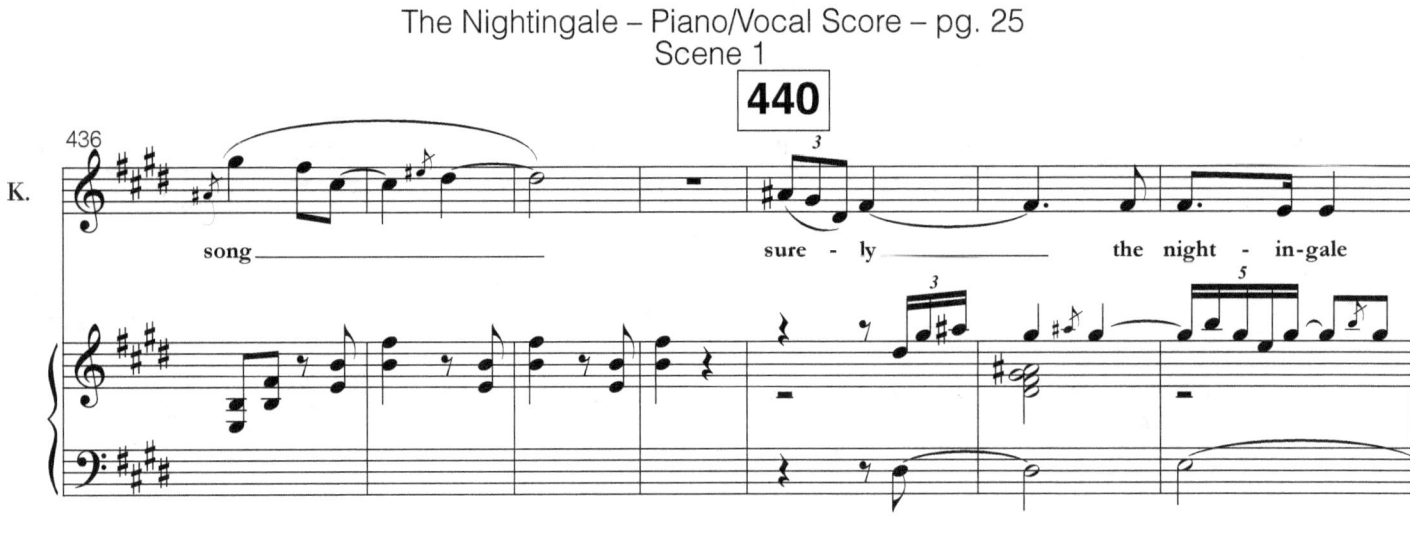

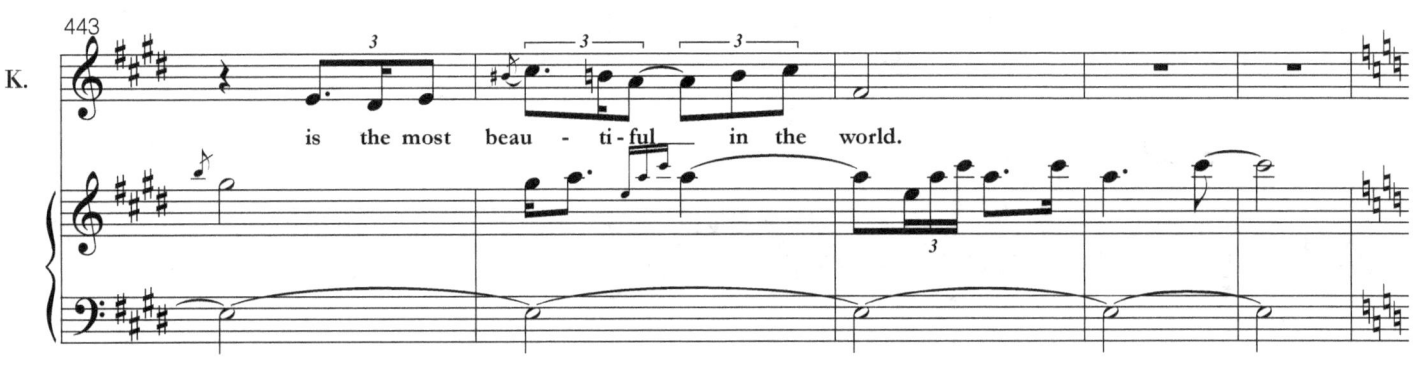

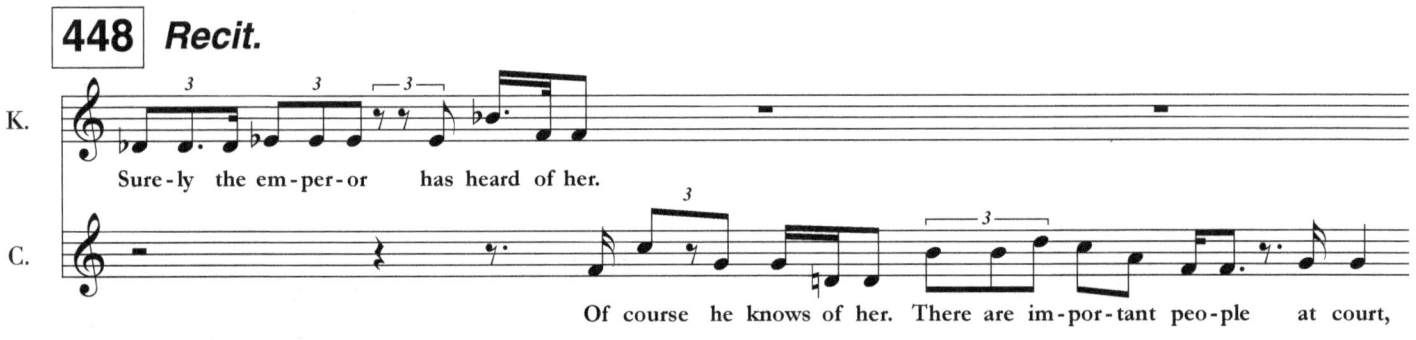

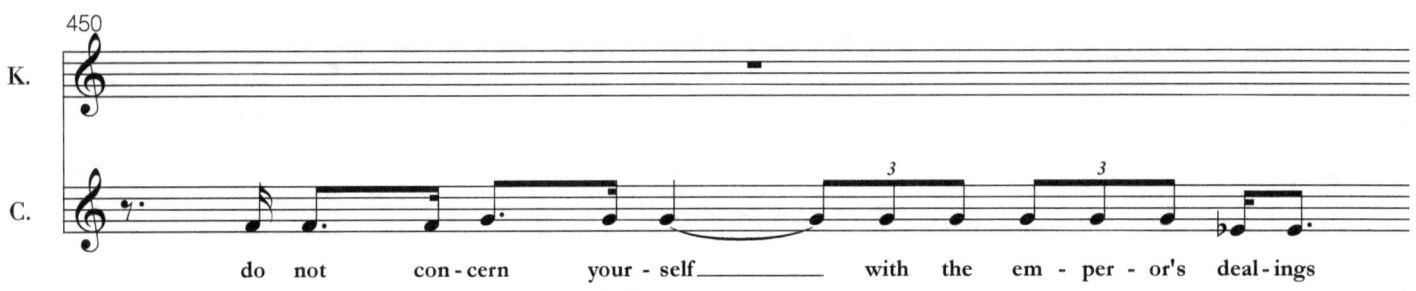

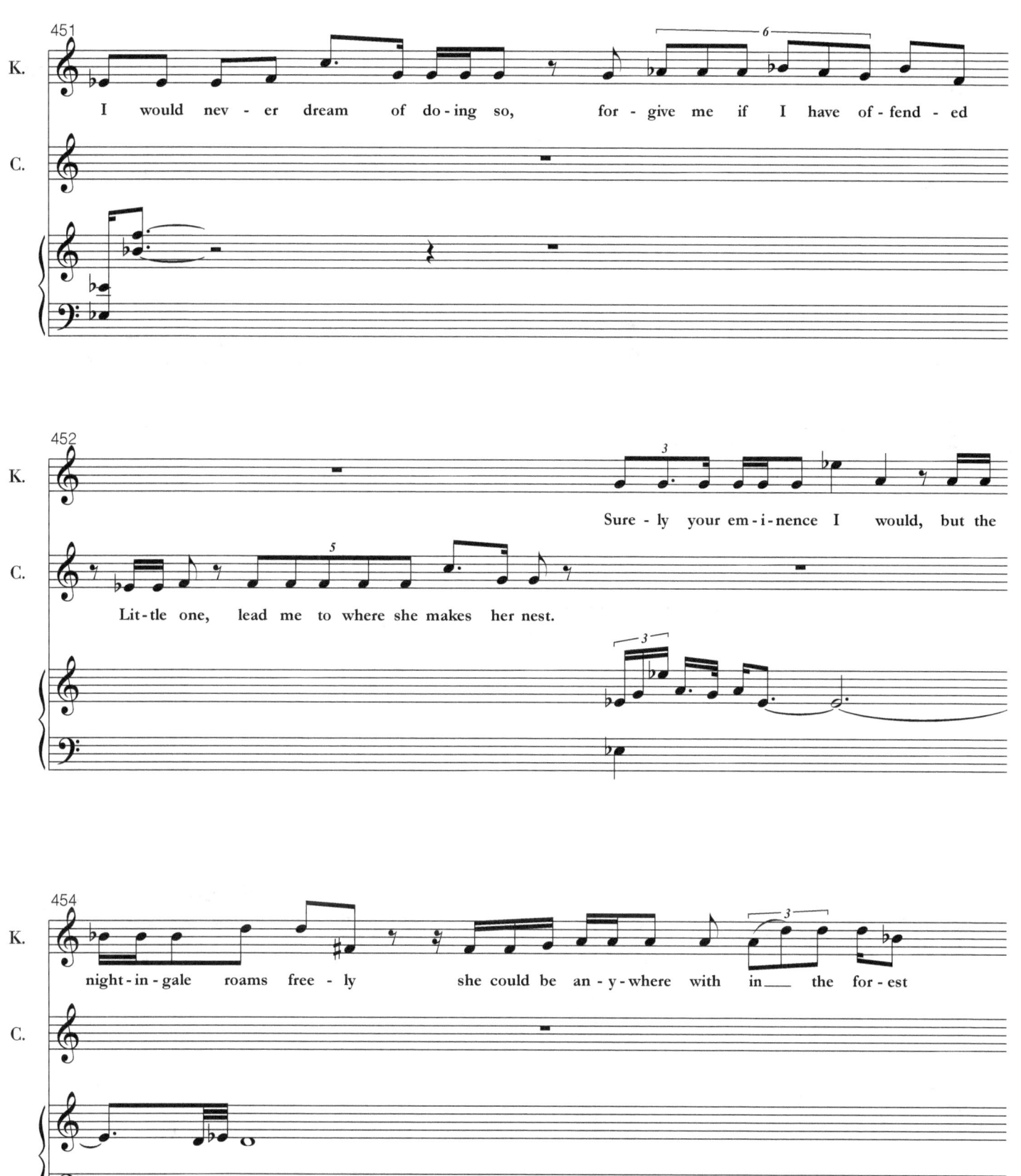

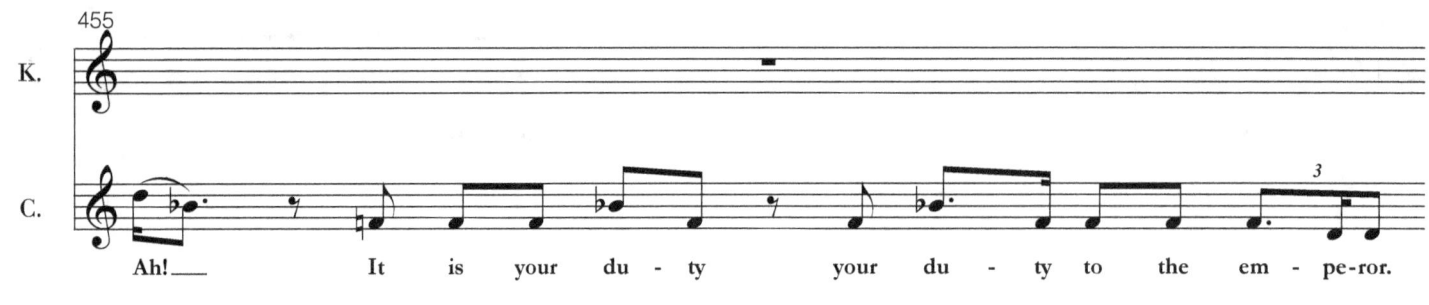

Ah!___ It is your du - ty your du - ty to the em - pe-ror.

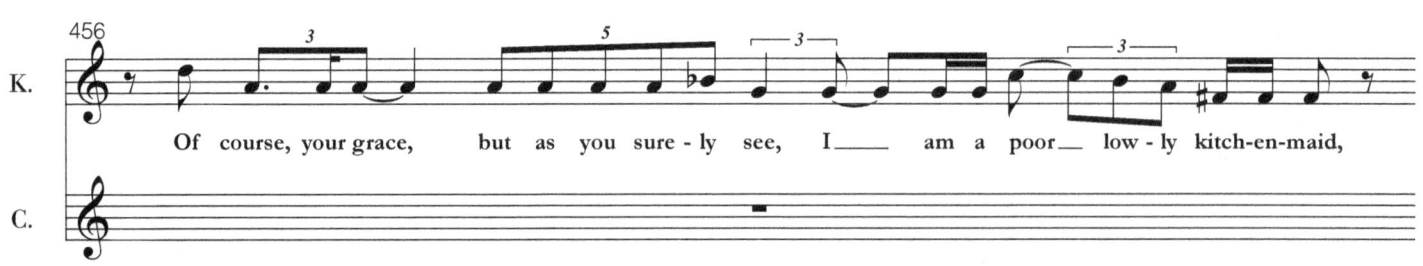

Of course, your grace, but as you sure - ly see, I___ am a poor___ low - ly kitch-en-maid,

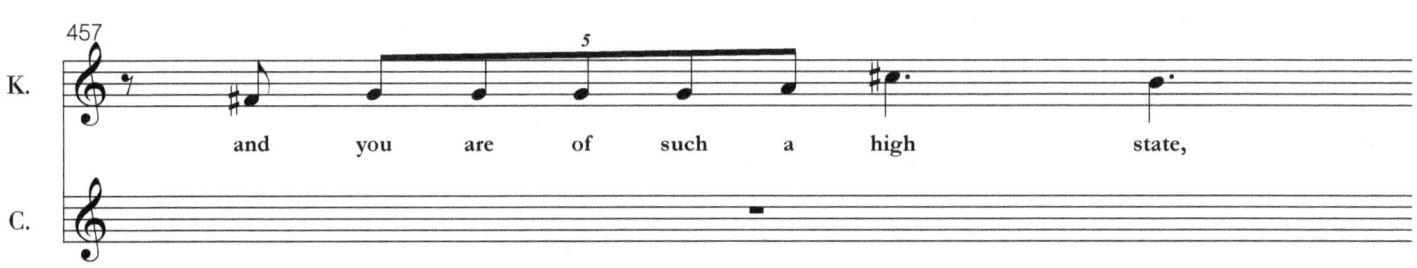

and you are of such a high state,

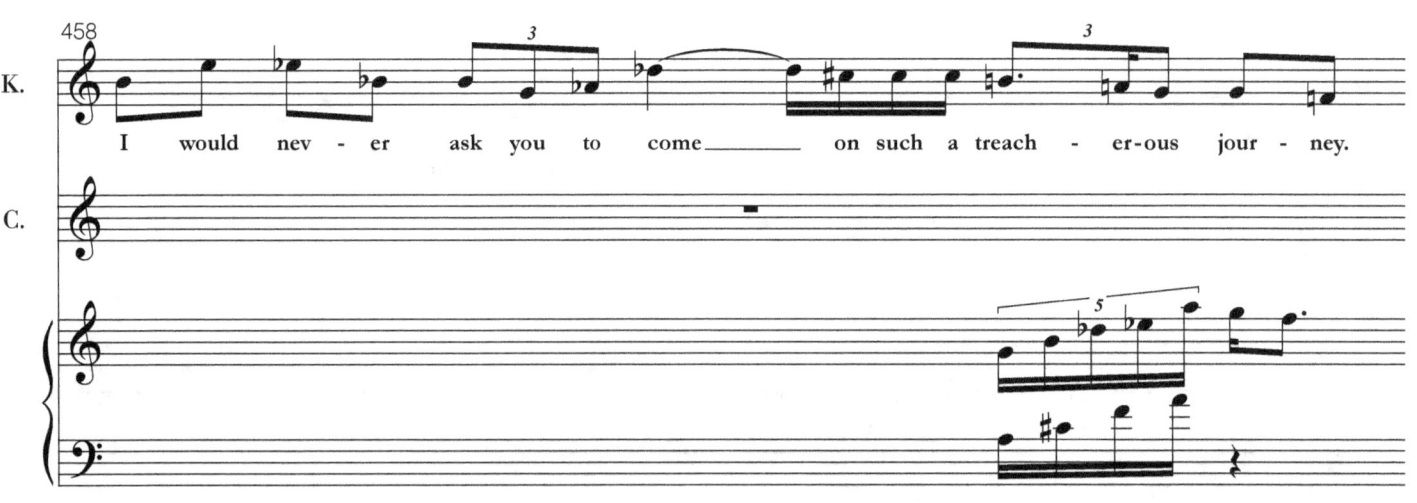

I would nev - er ask you to come_____ on such a treach - er-ous jour - ney.

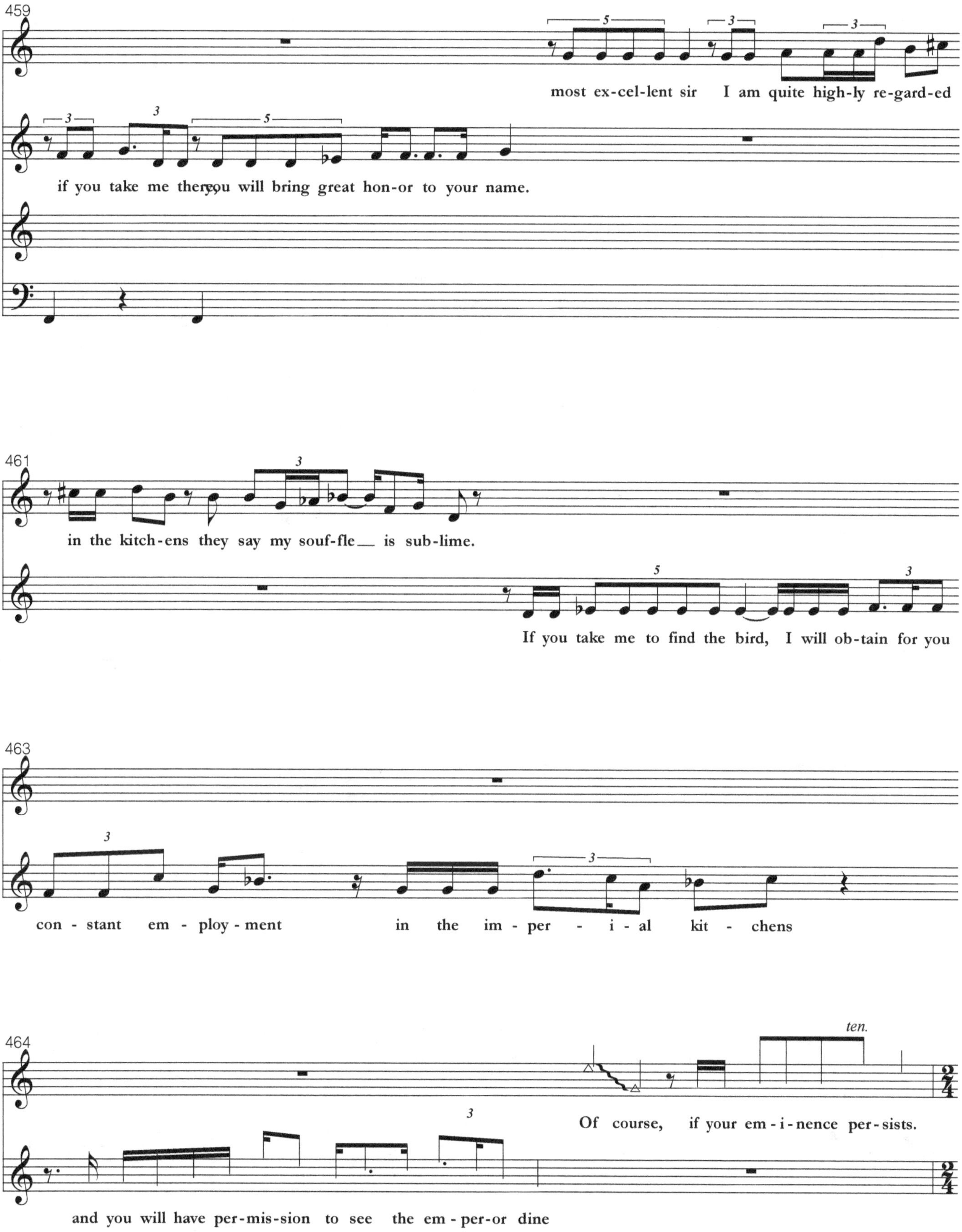

459

K. (rest)

most ex-cel-lent sir   I am quite high-ly re-gard-ed

C. if you take me there you will bring great hon-or to your name.

461

K. in the kitch-ens they say my souf-fle __ is sub-lime.

C. If you take me to find the bird, I will ob-tain for you

463

K. (rest)

C. con - stant   em - ploy - ment   in   the   im - per - i - al   kit - chens

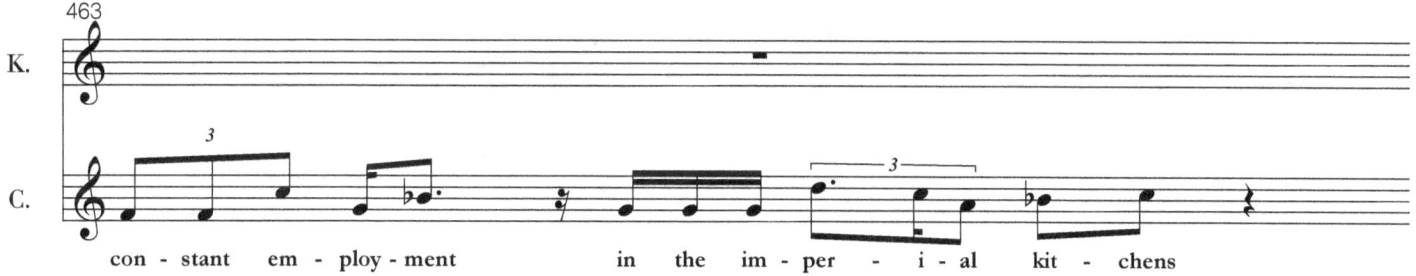

464

ten.

K. Of course,   if your em - i - nence per - sists.

C. and you will have per-mis-sion to see   the em-per-or dine

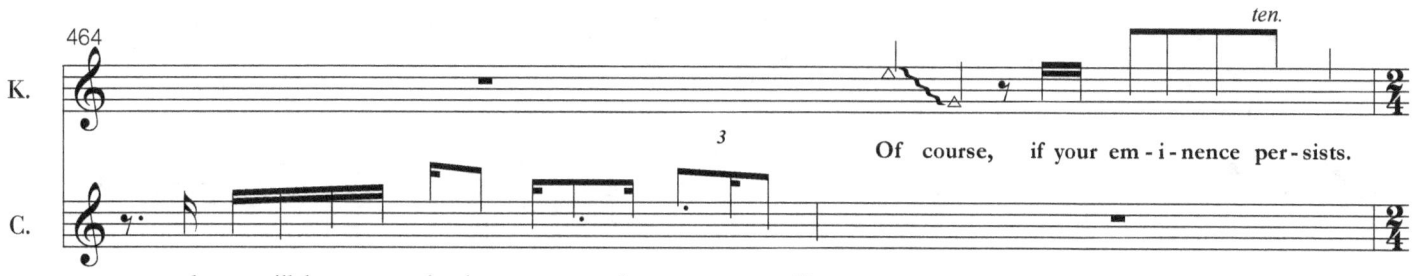

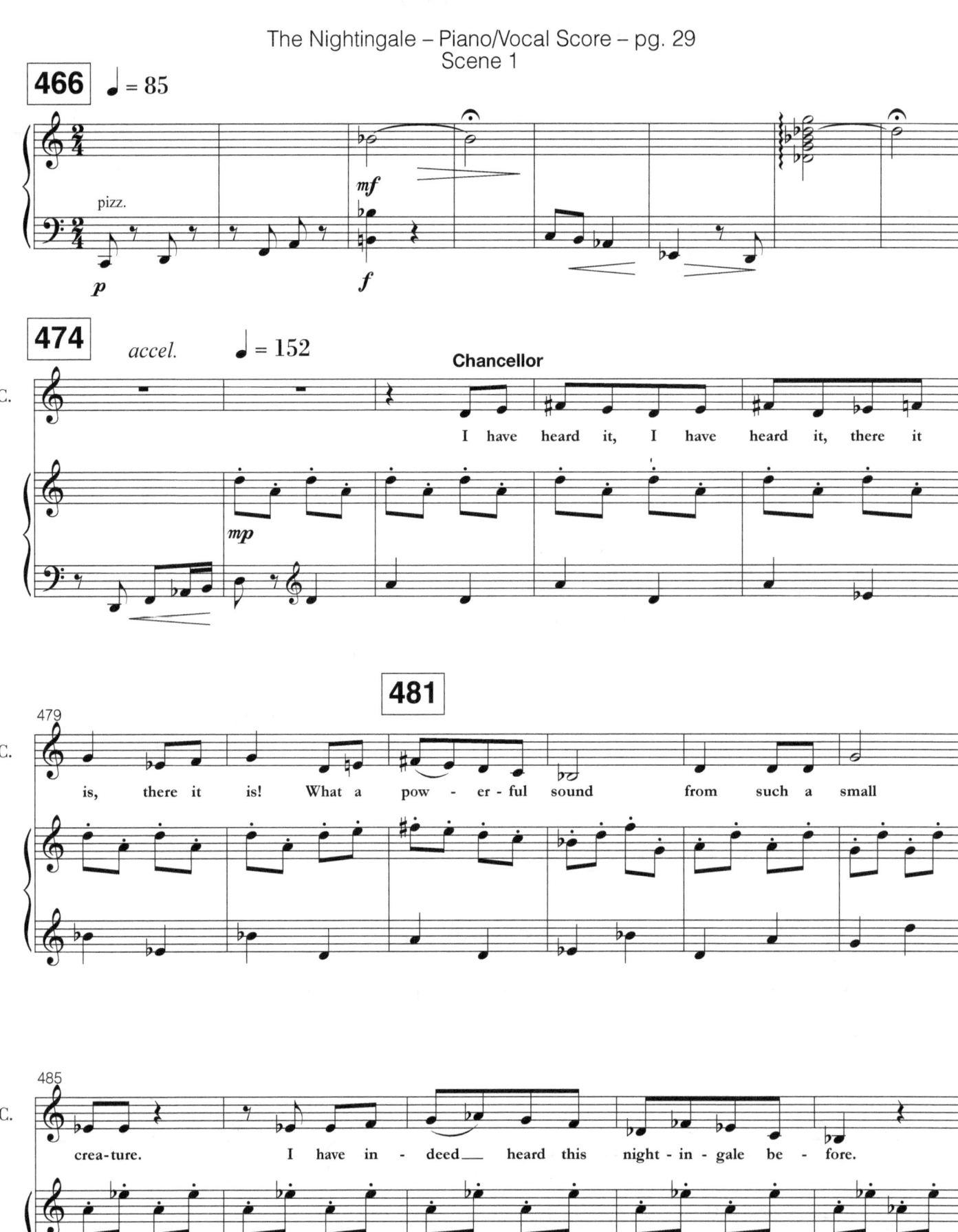

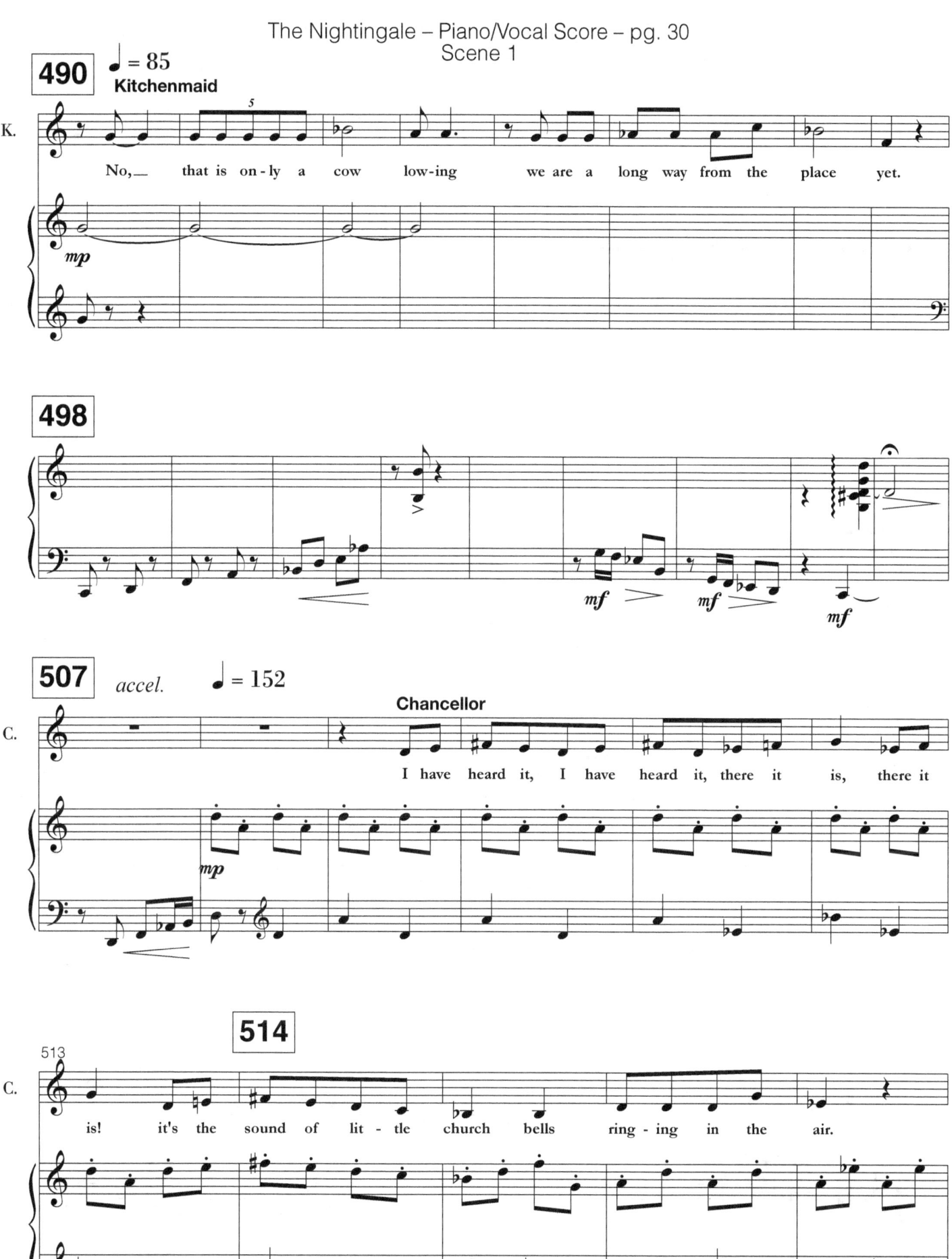

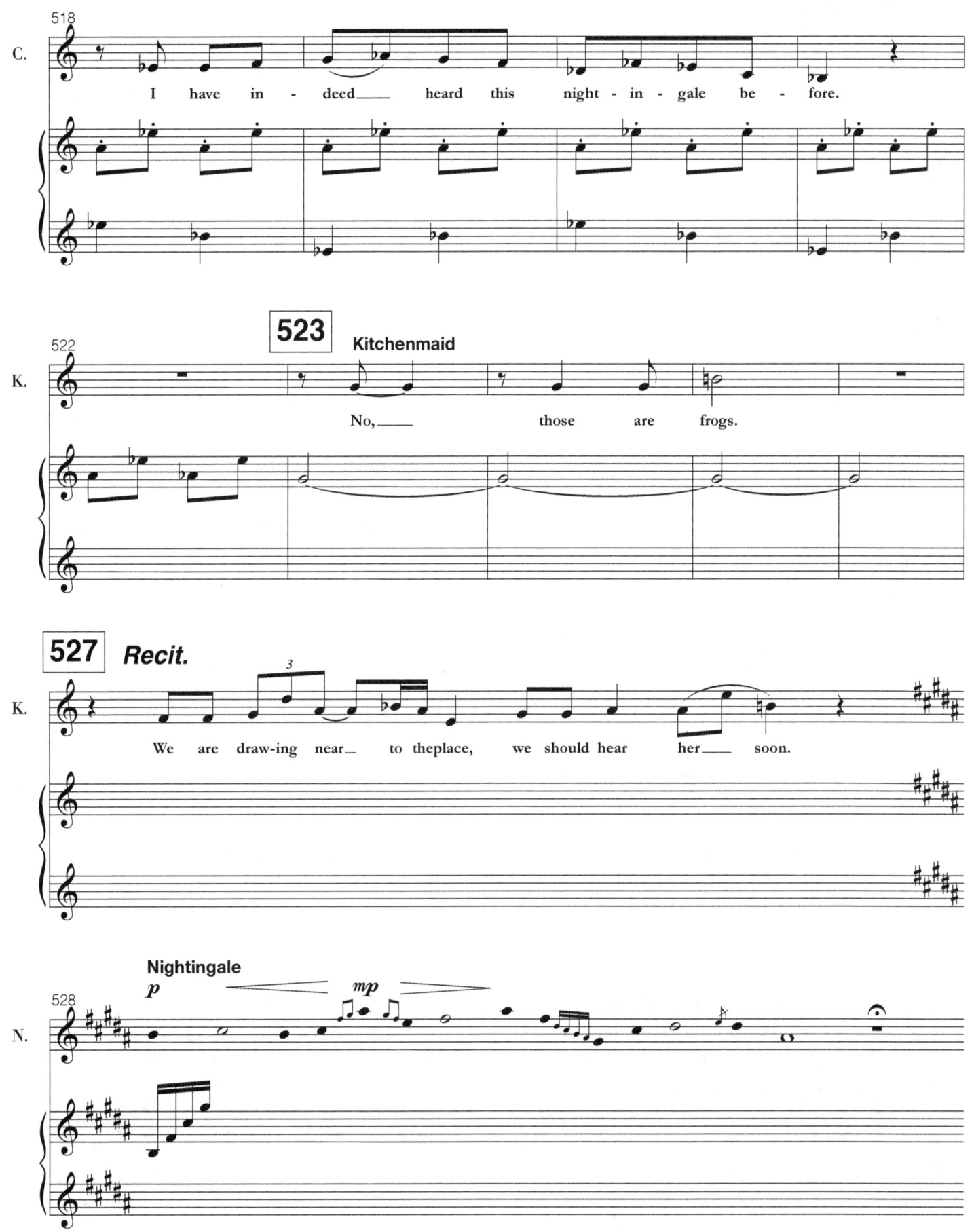

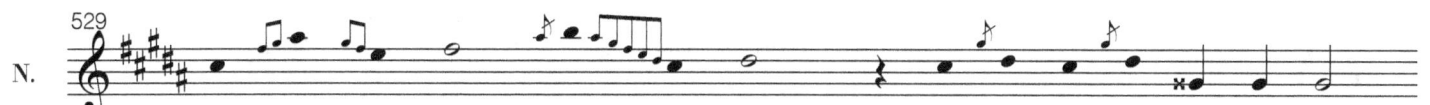

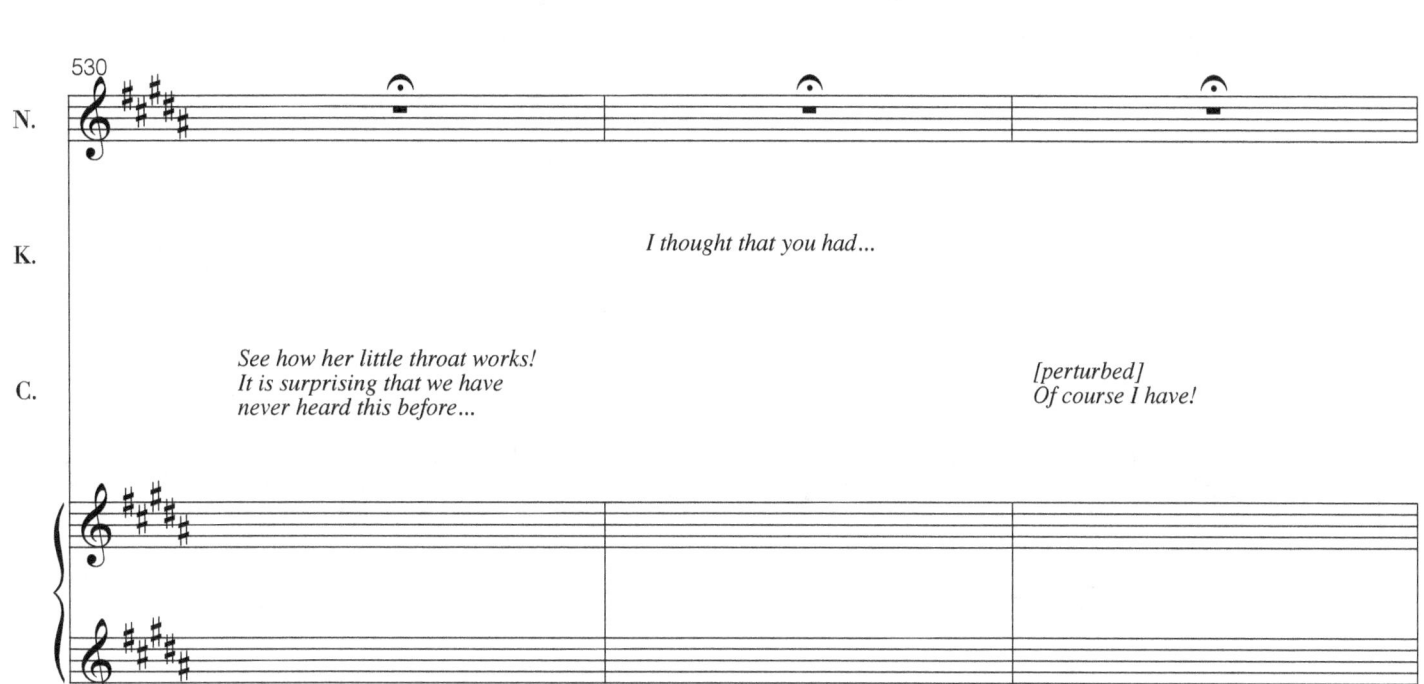

K.

I thought that you had...

C.

See how her little throat works!
It is surprising that we have
never heard this before...

[perturbed]
Of course I have!

533

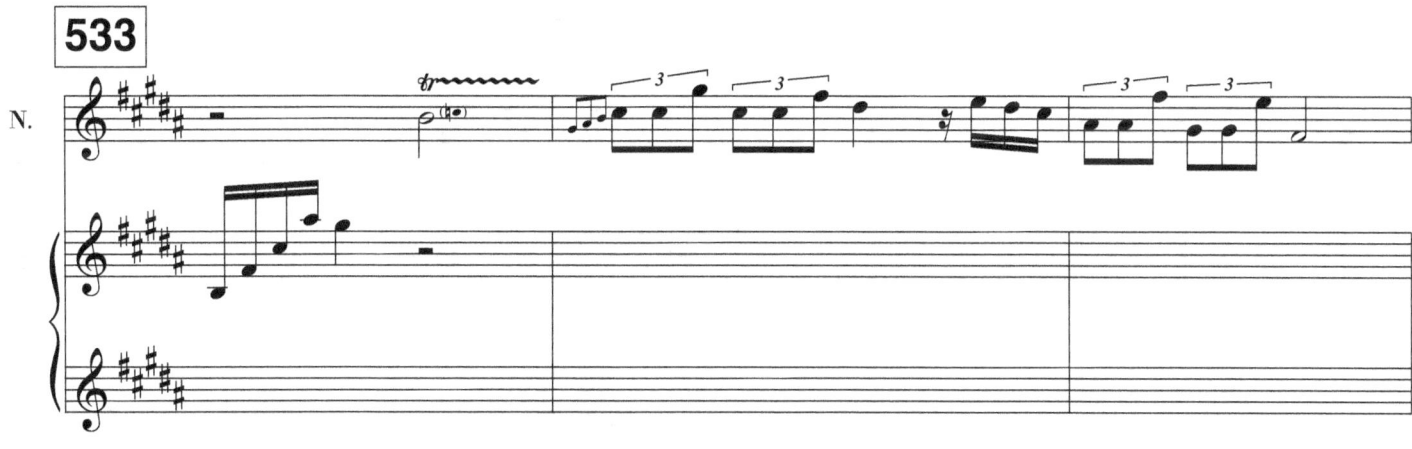

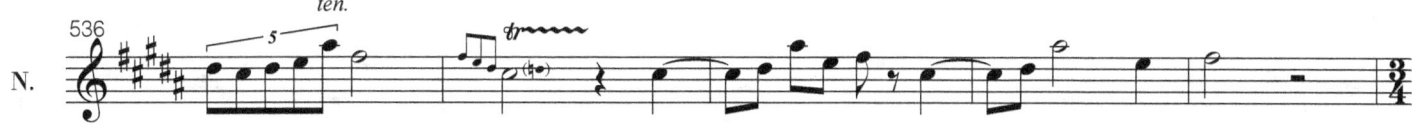

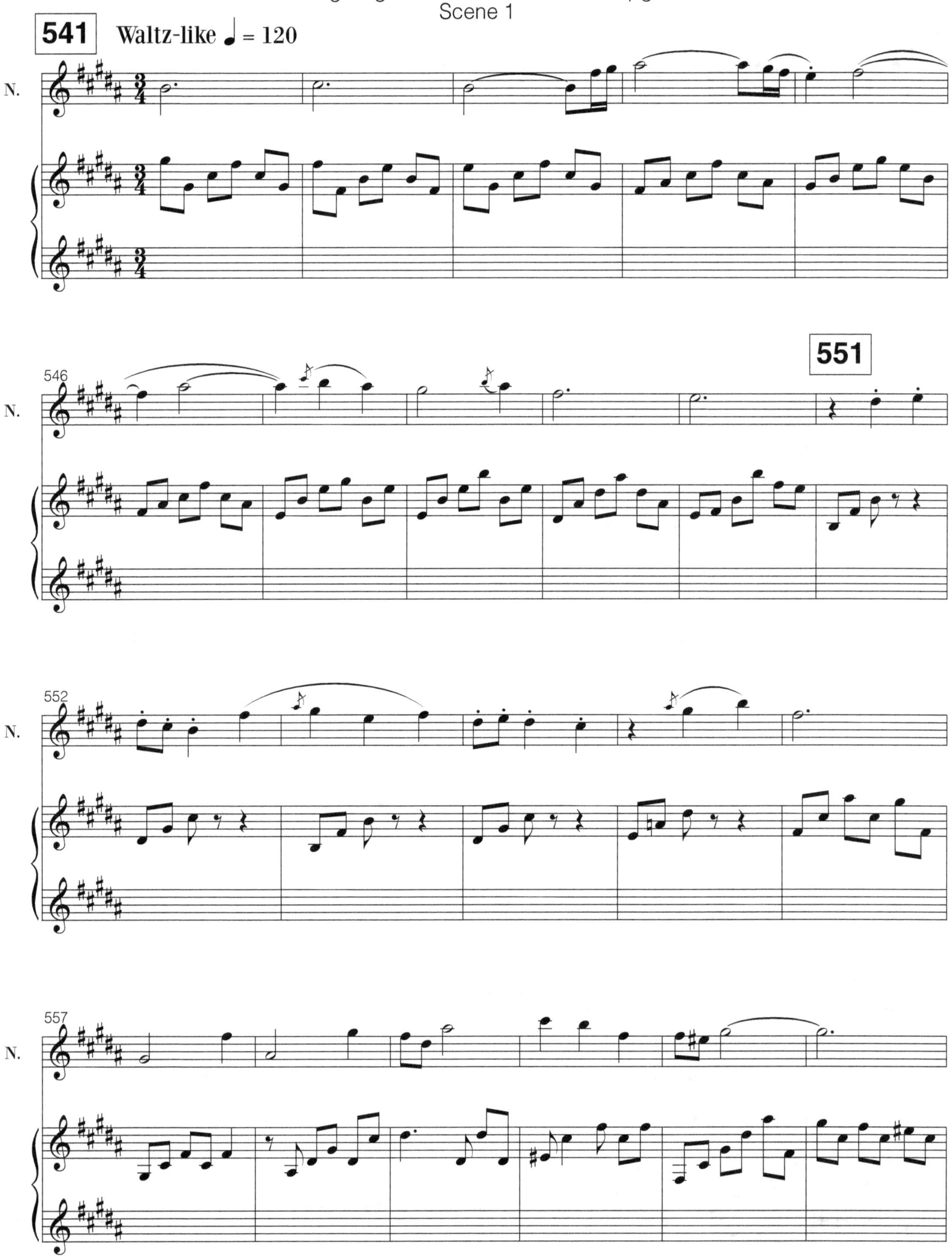
541
Waltz-like ♩ = 120
N.
546
551
552
557

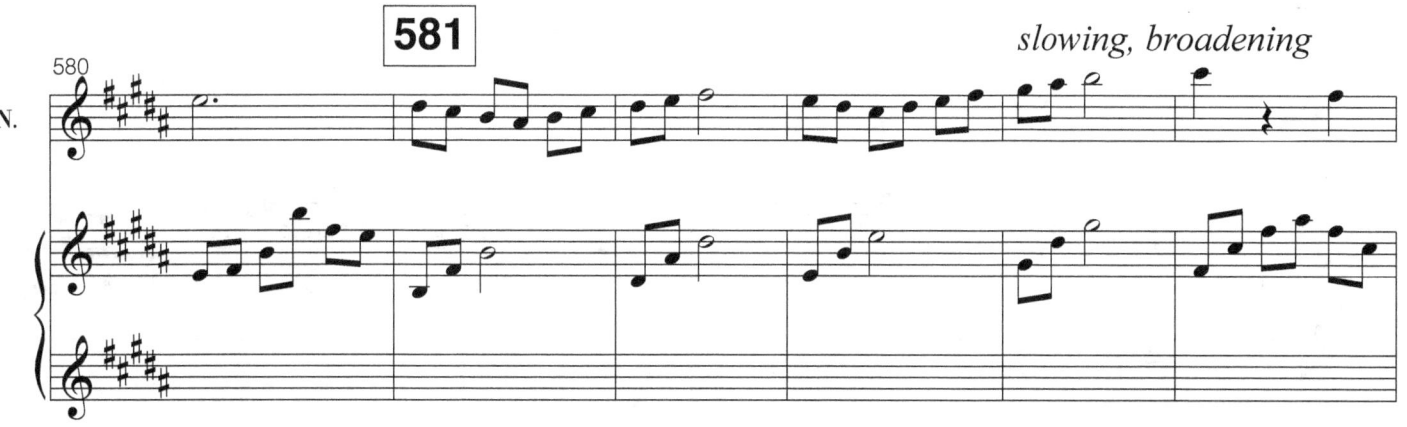

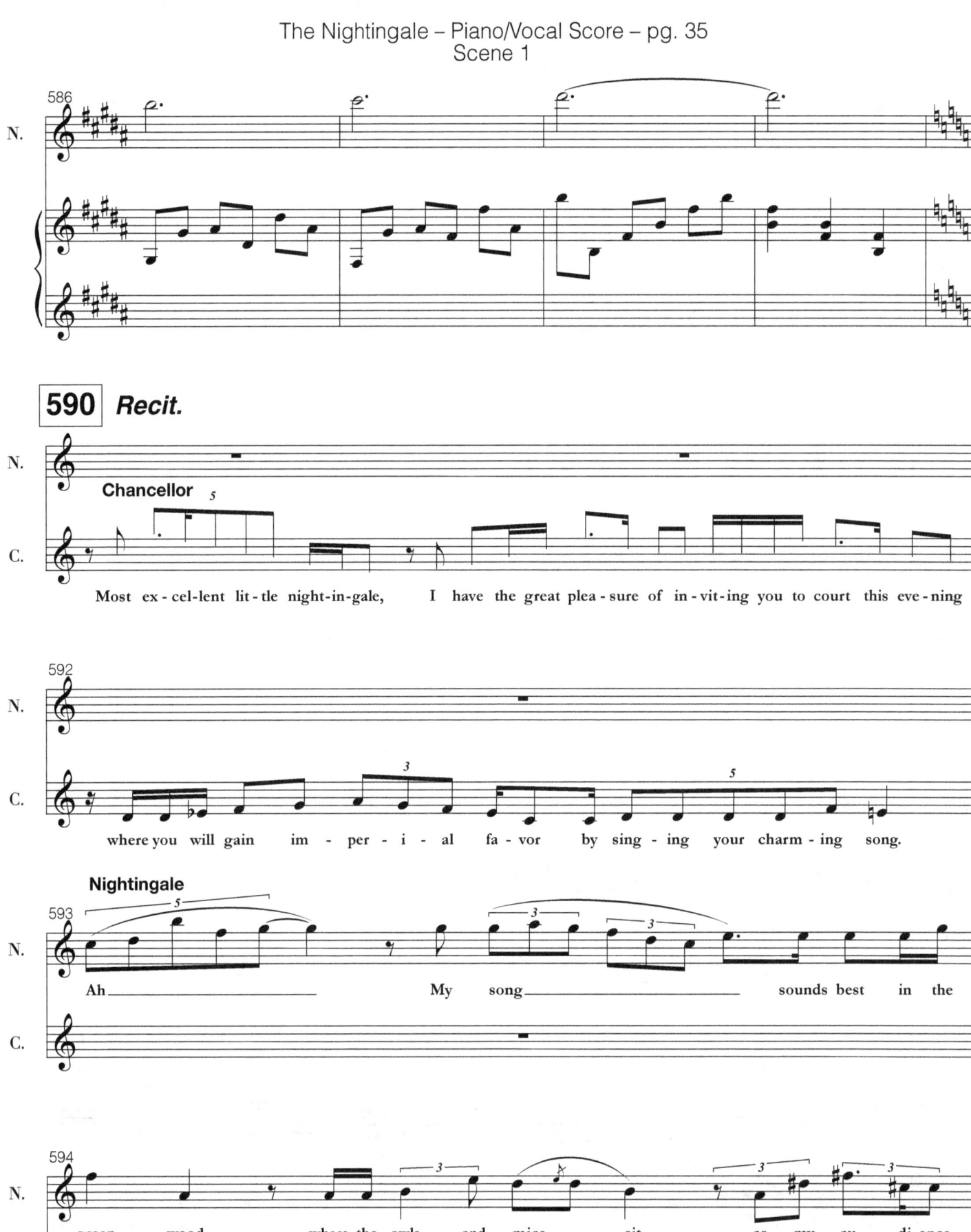

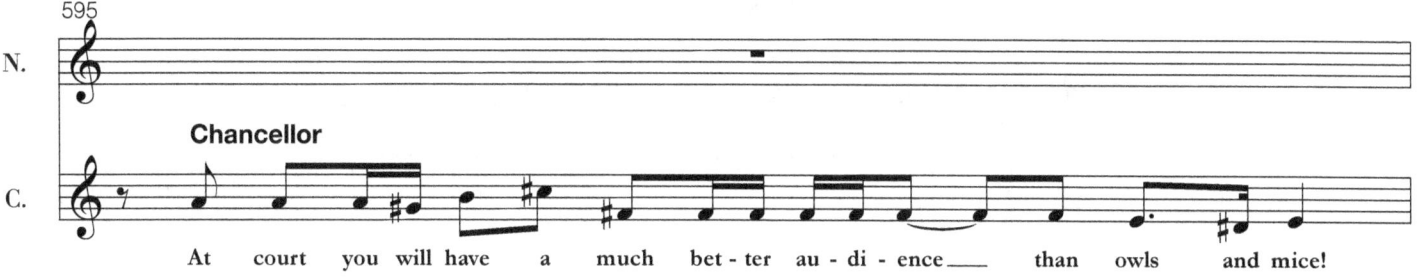

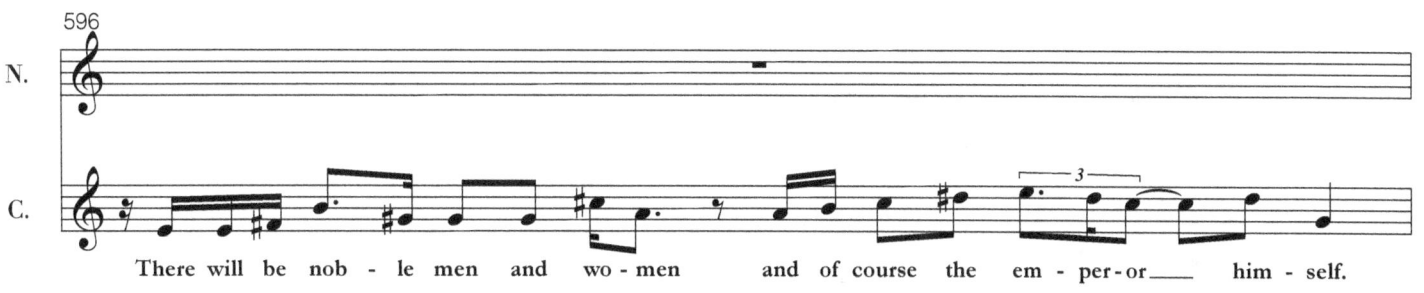

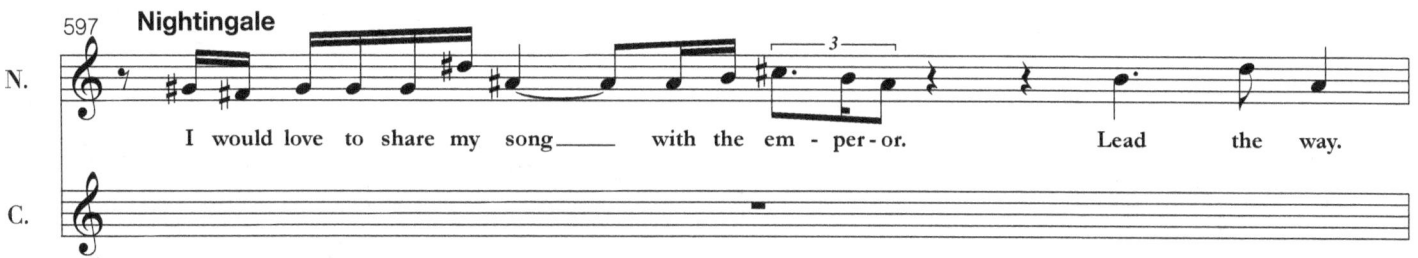

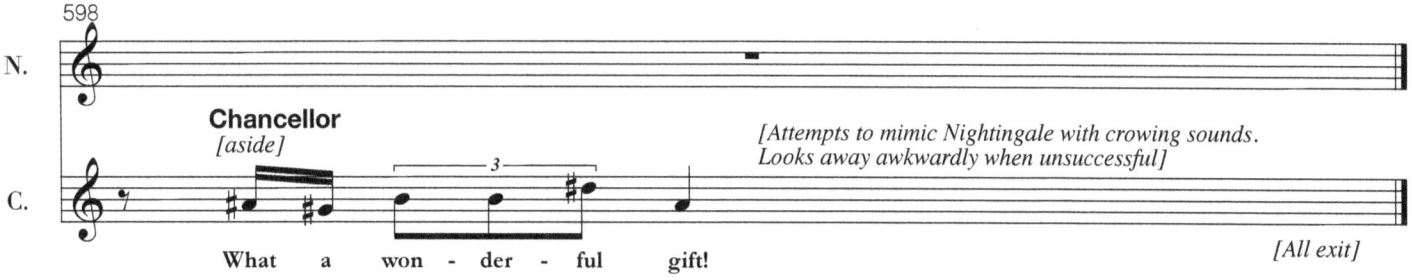

[End of Scene 1]

Scene 2

The Imperial Palace
Nightingale, Emperor, Chancellor, Mechanical Nightingale

The emperor and chancellor are sitting comfortably in the scene, enjoying a performance by the nightingale. The nightingale should be front-and-center as if she is nearing the end of an enrapturing performance.

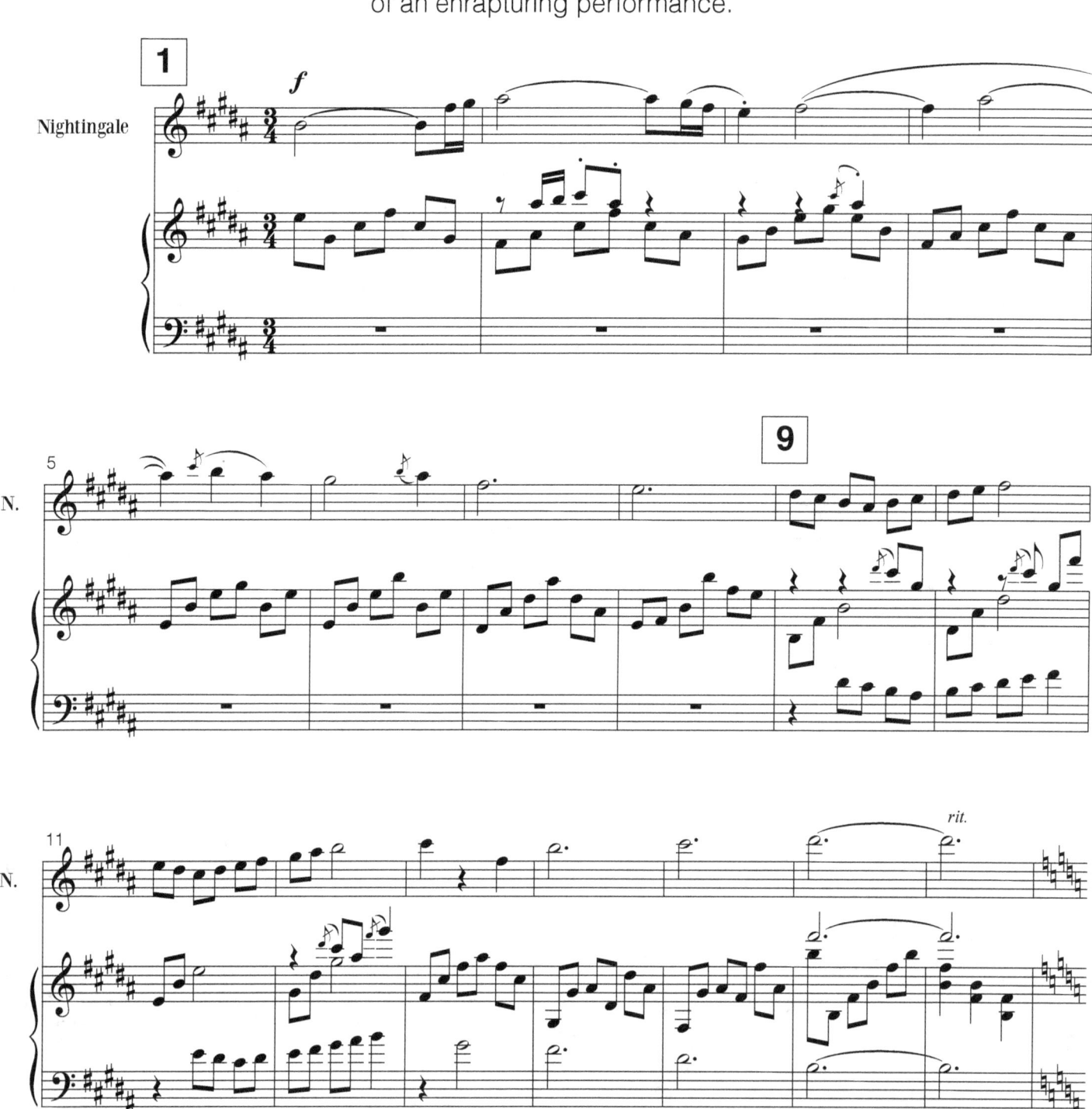

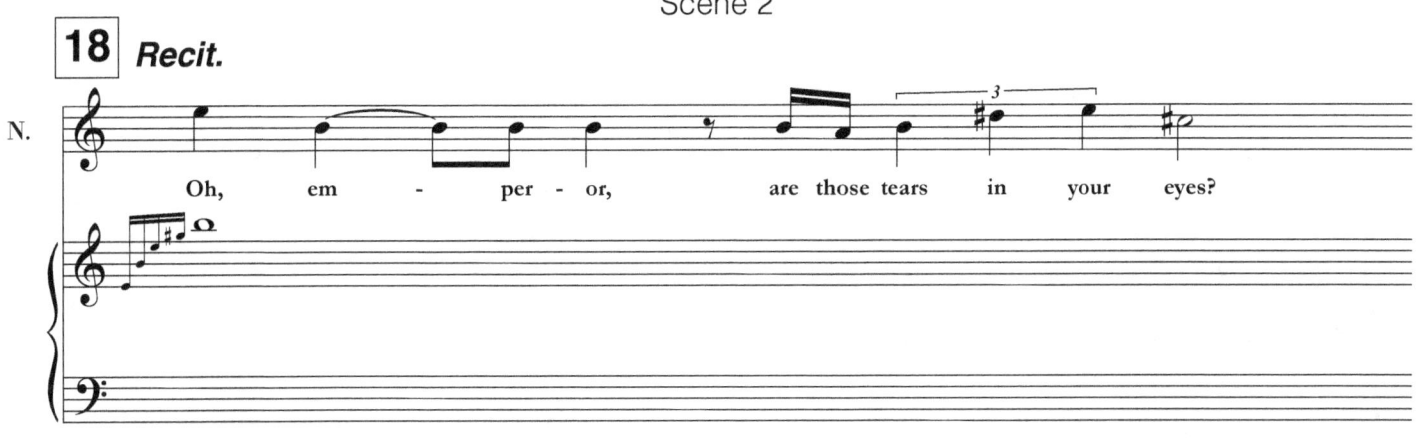

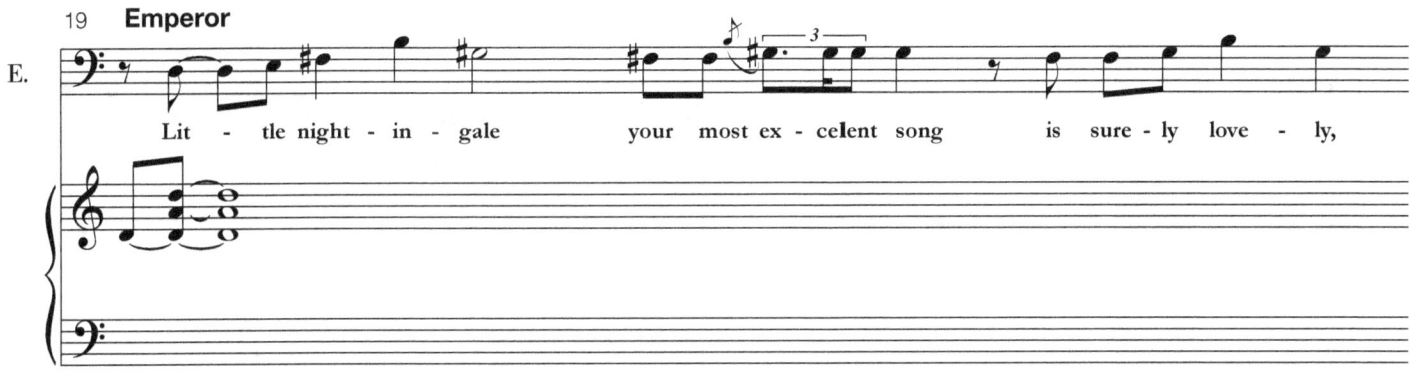

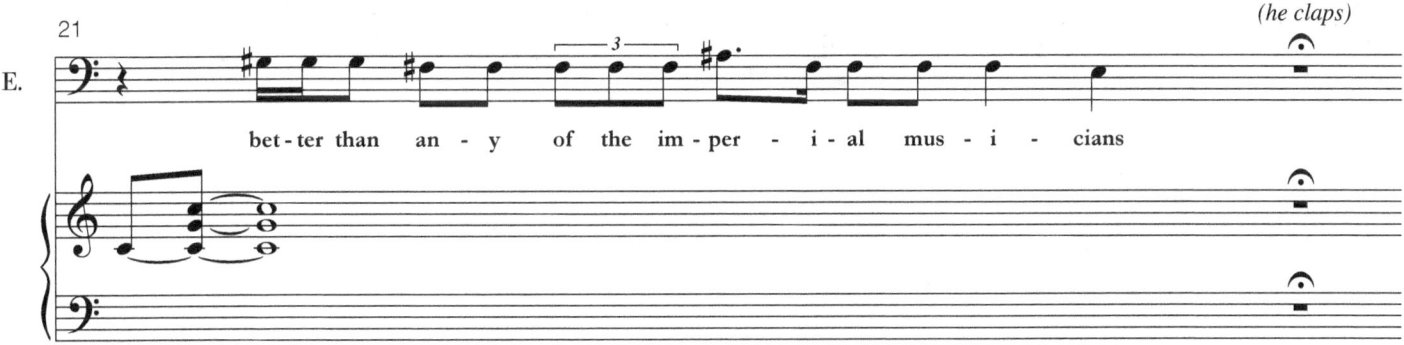

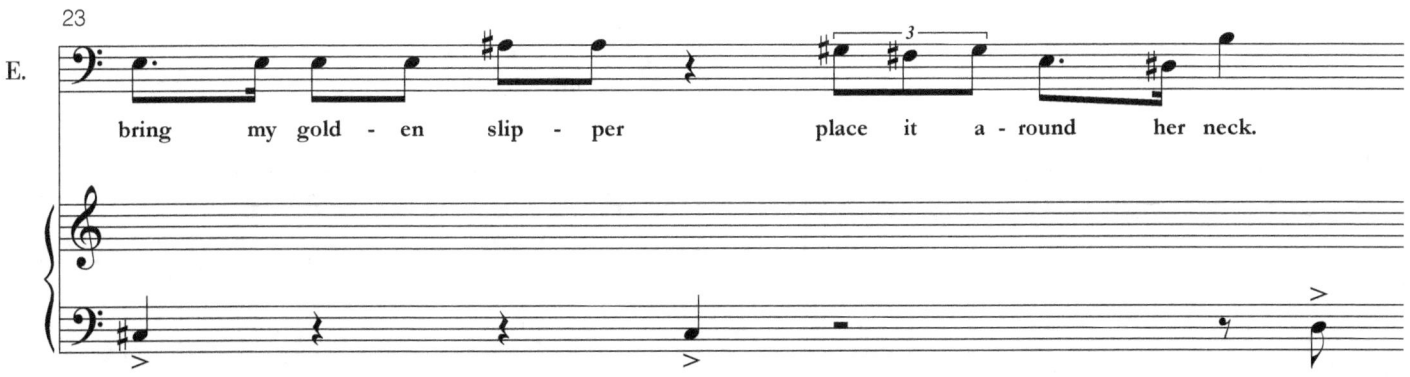

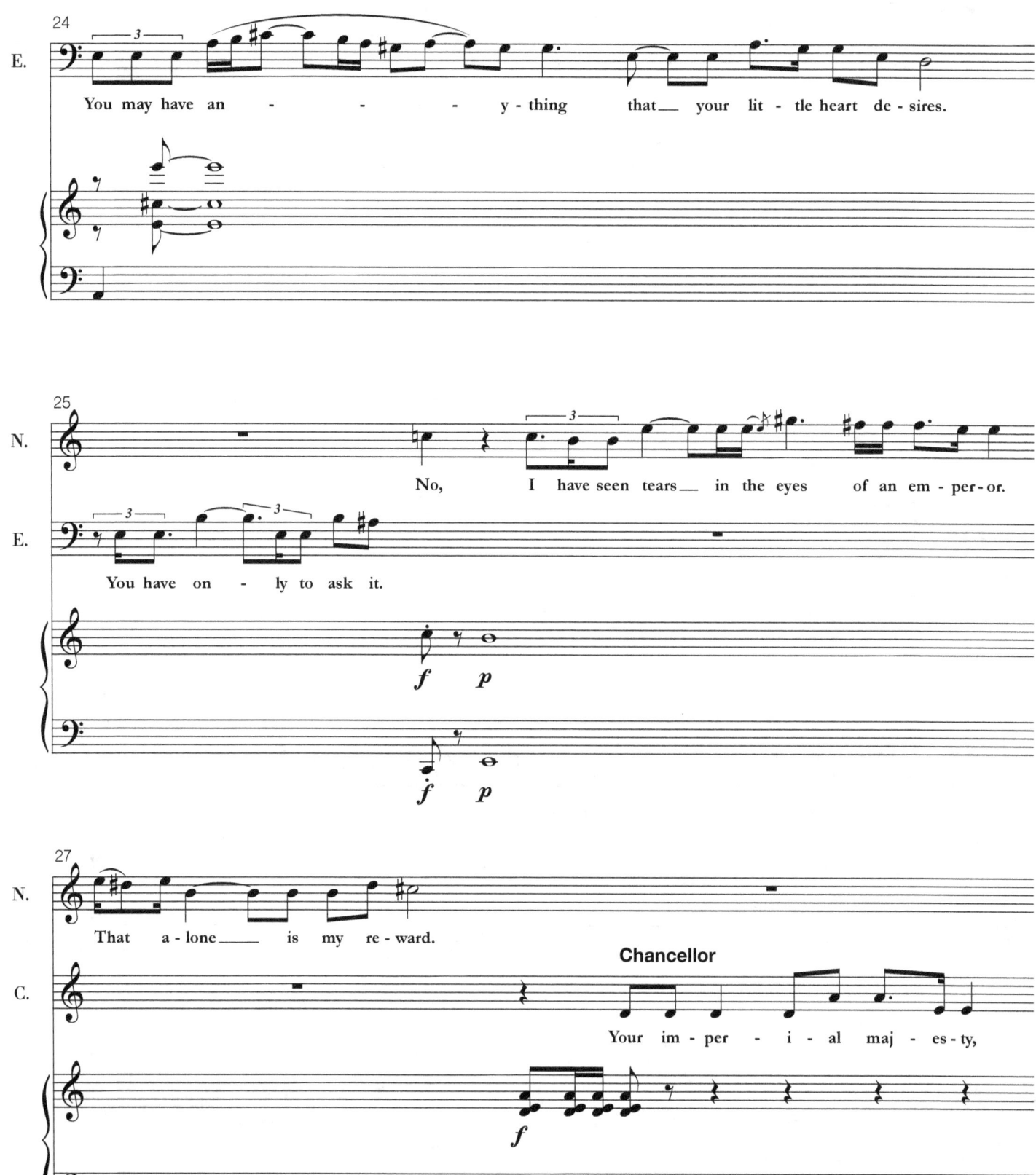

Scene 2

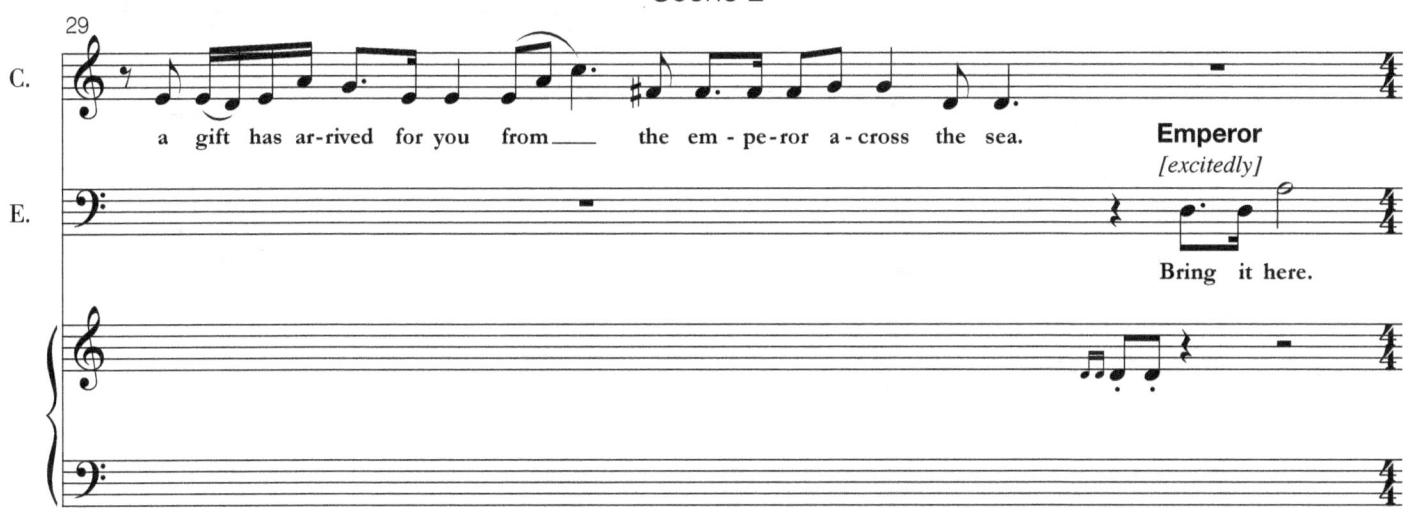

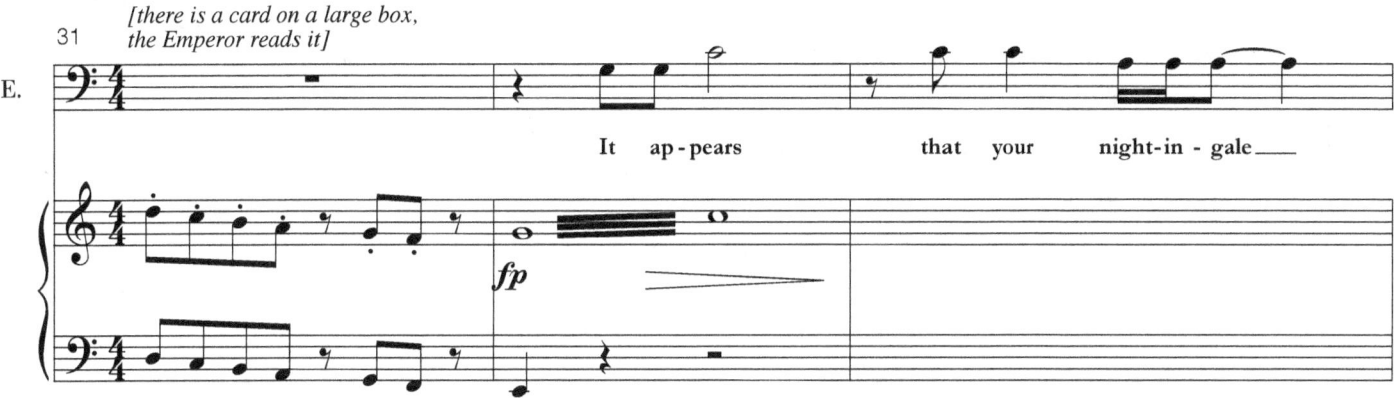

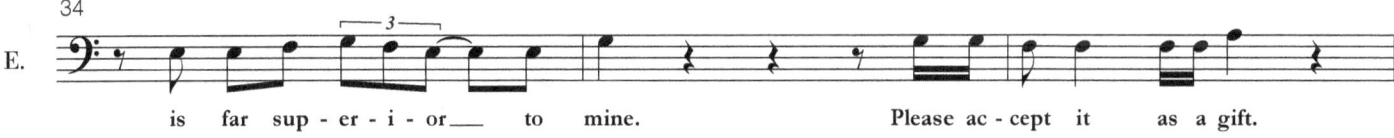

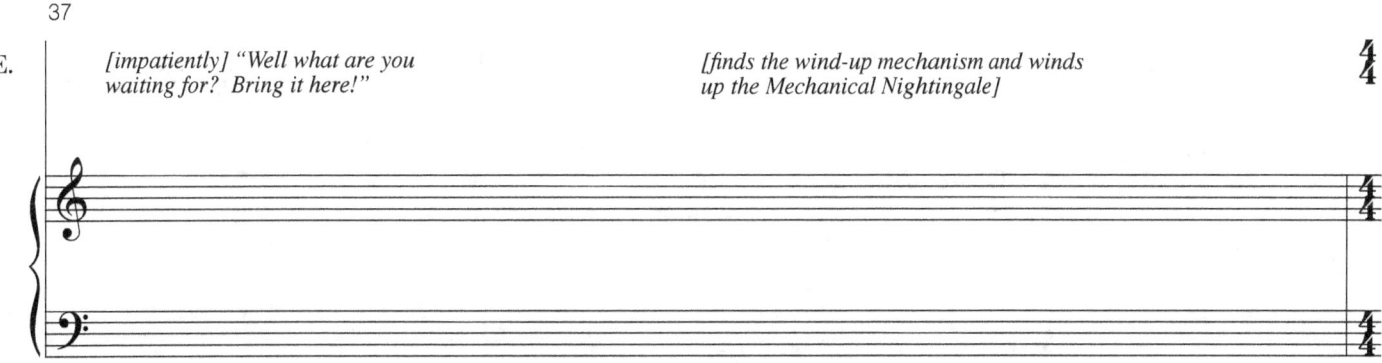

Scene 2

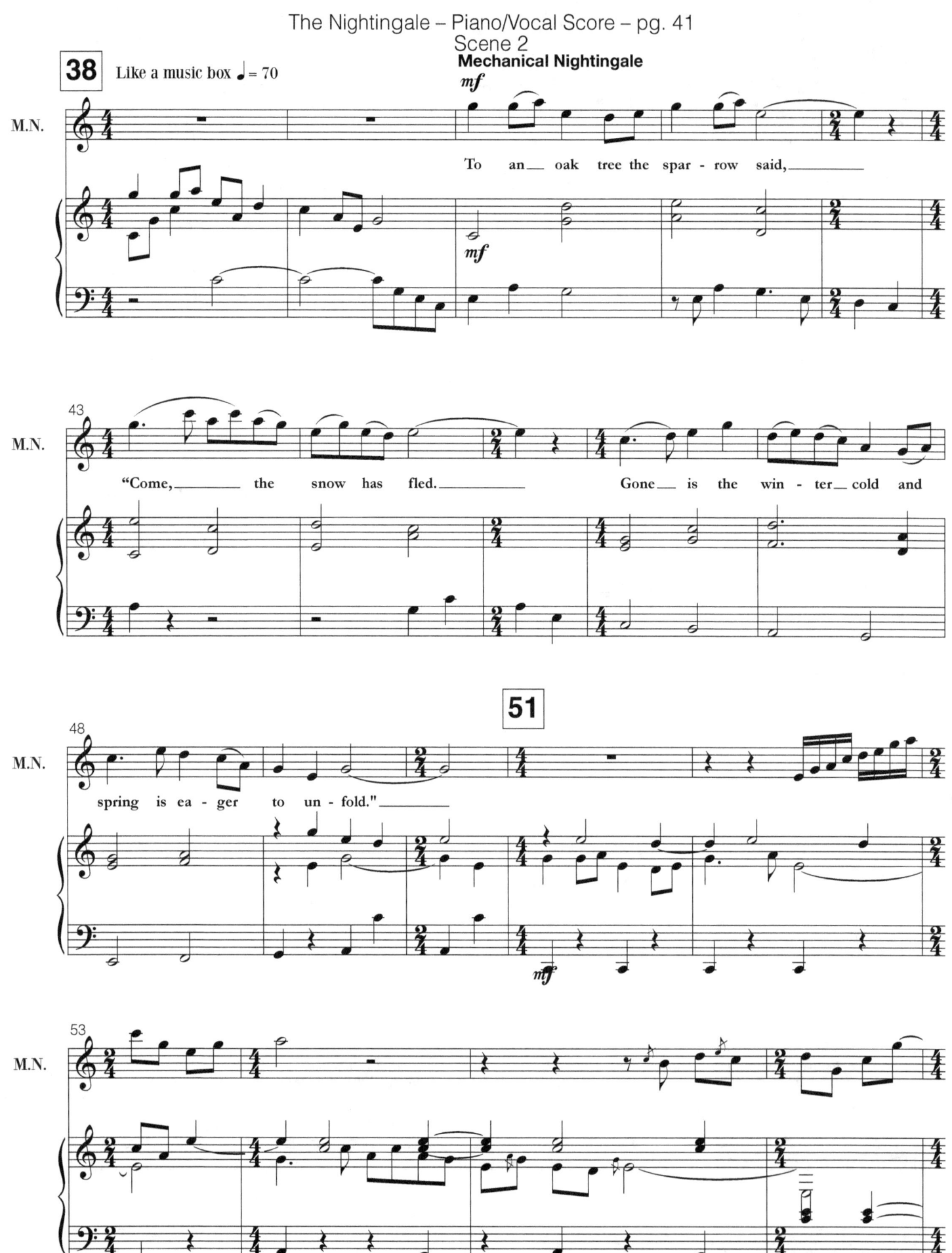

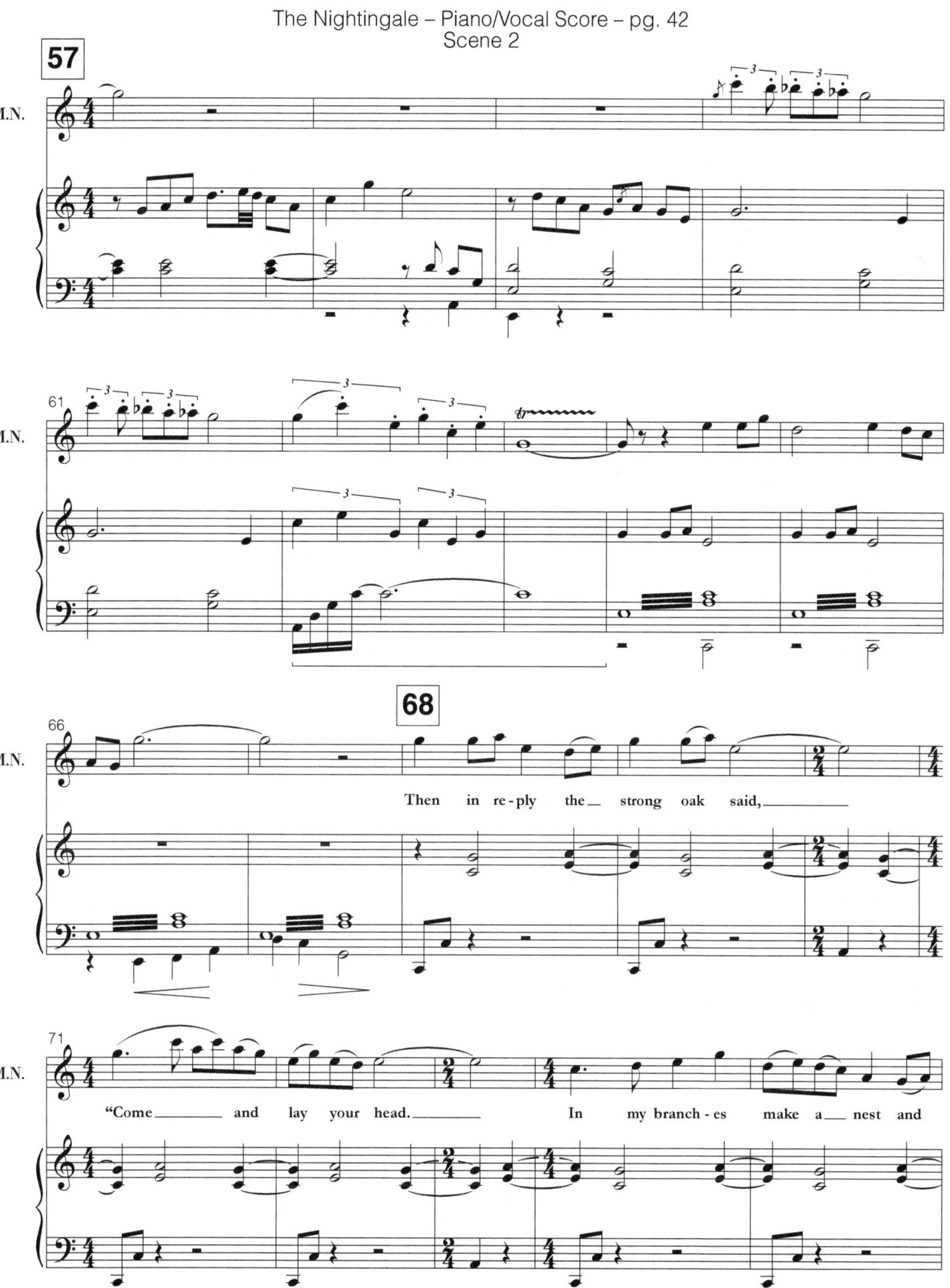

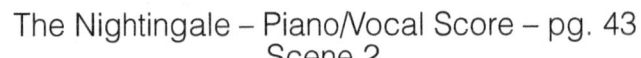

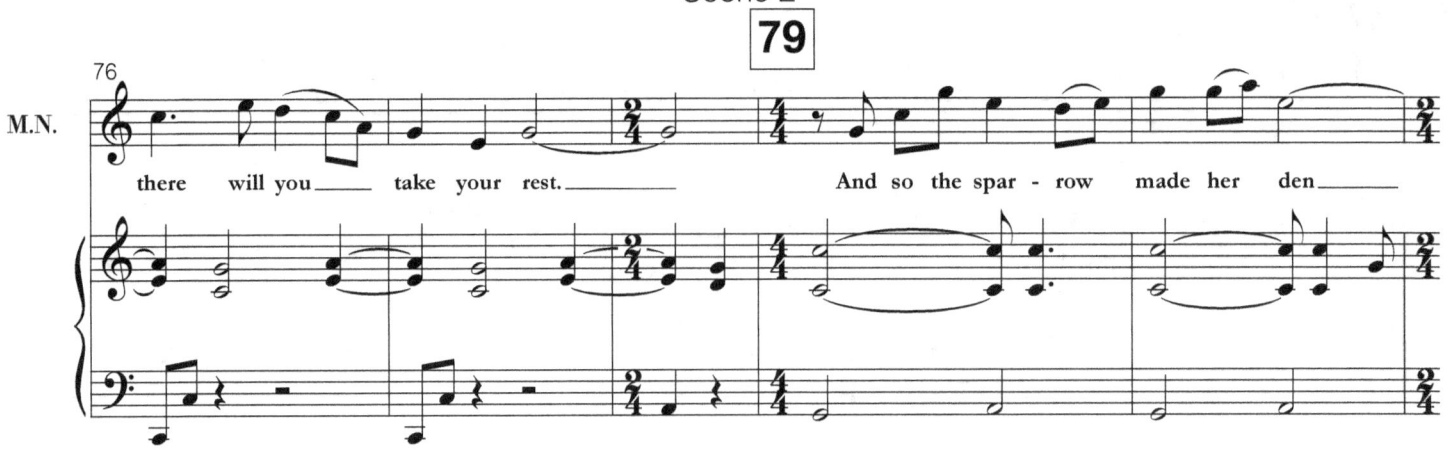

there will you___ take your rest.___ And so the spar - row made her den___

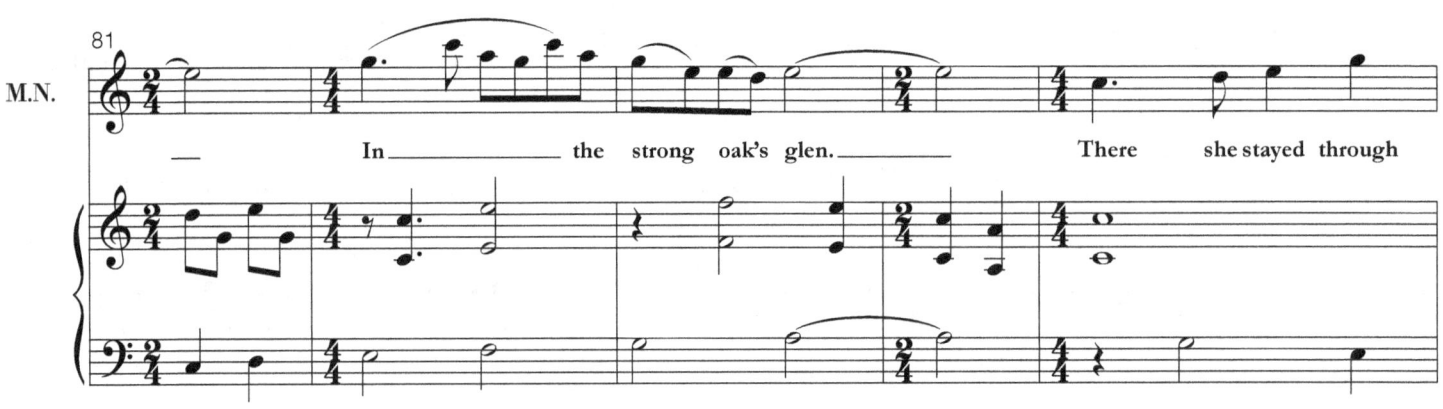

___ In___ the strong oak's glen.___ There she stayed through

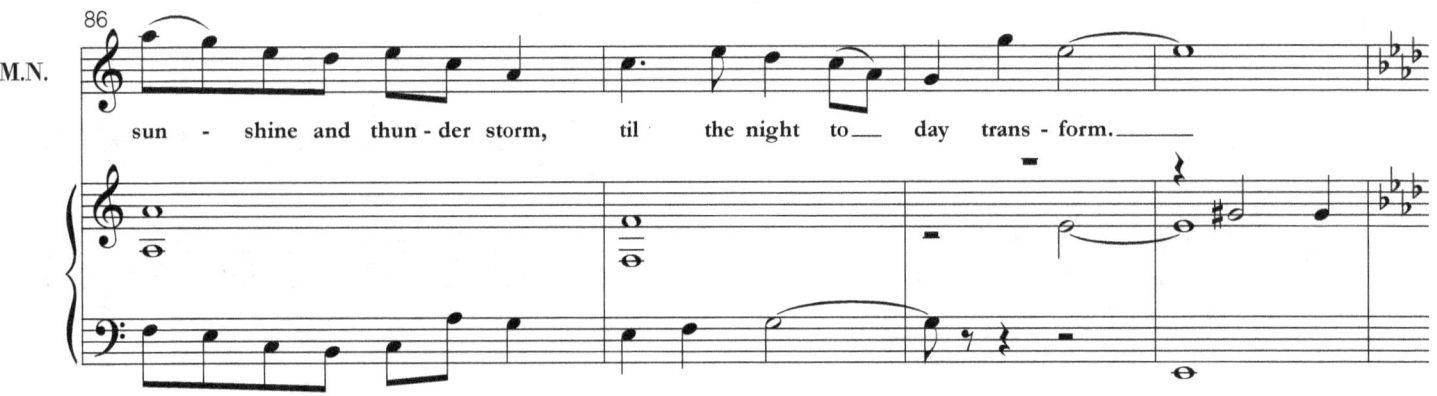

sun - shine and thun - der storm, til the night to___ day trans - form.___

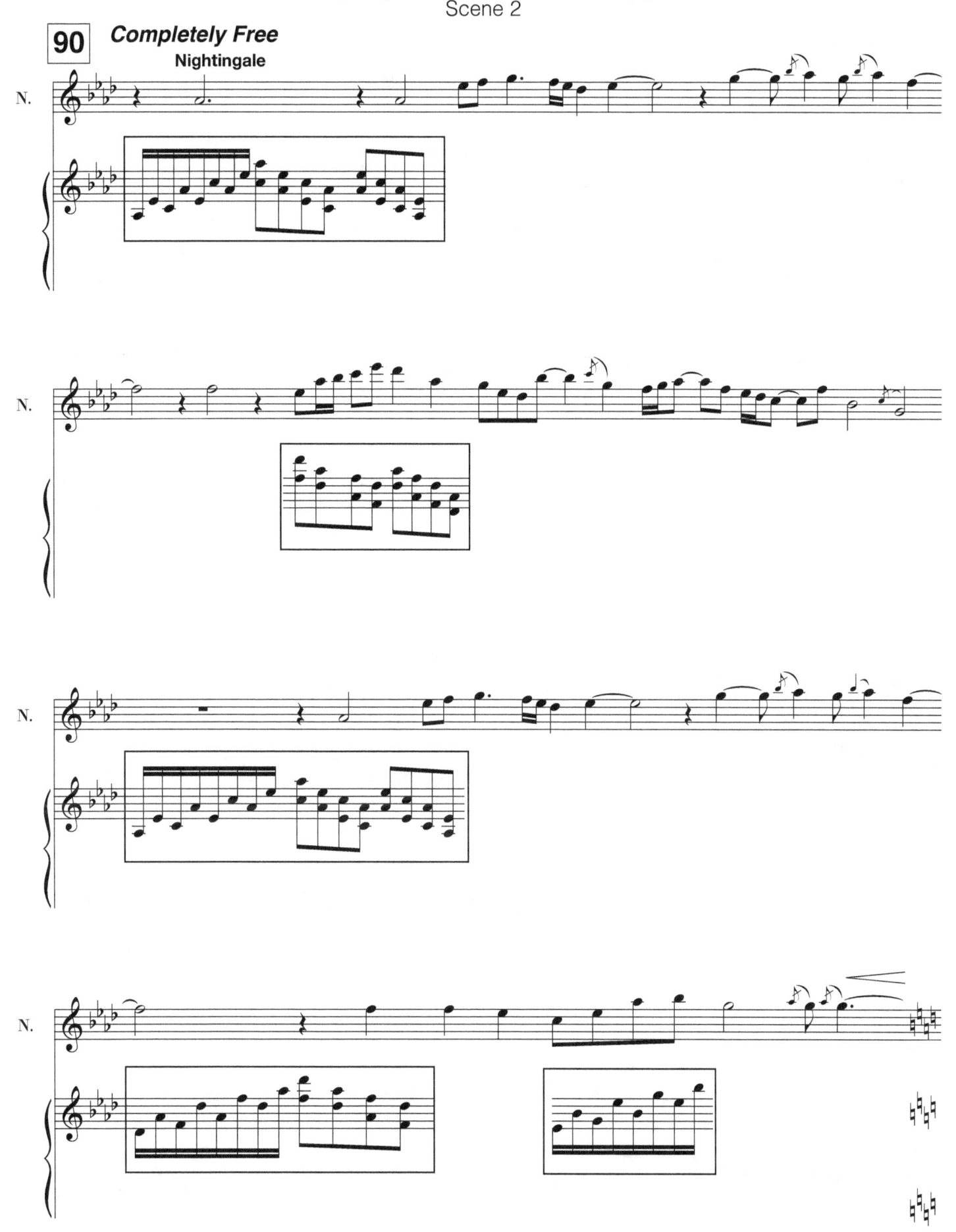

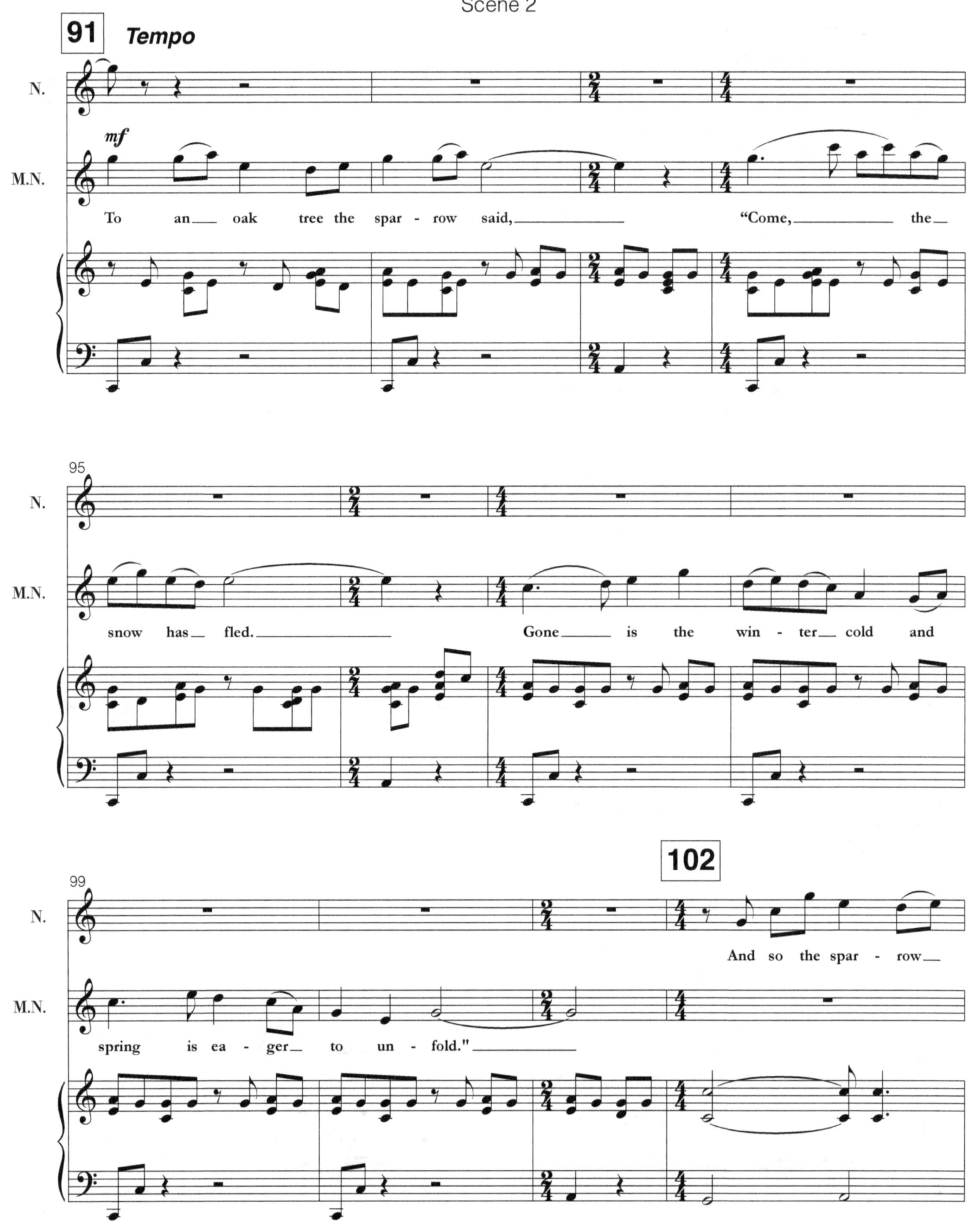

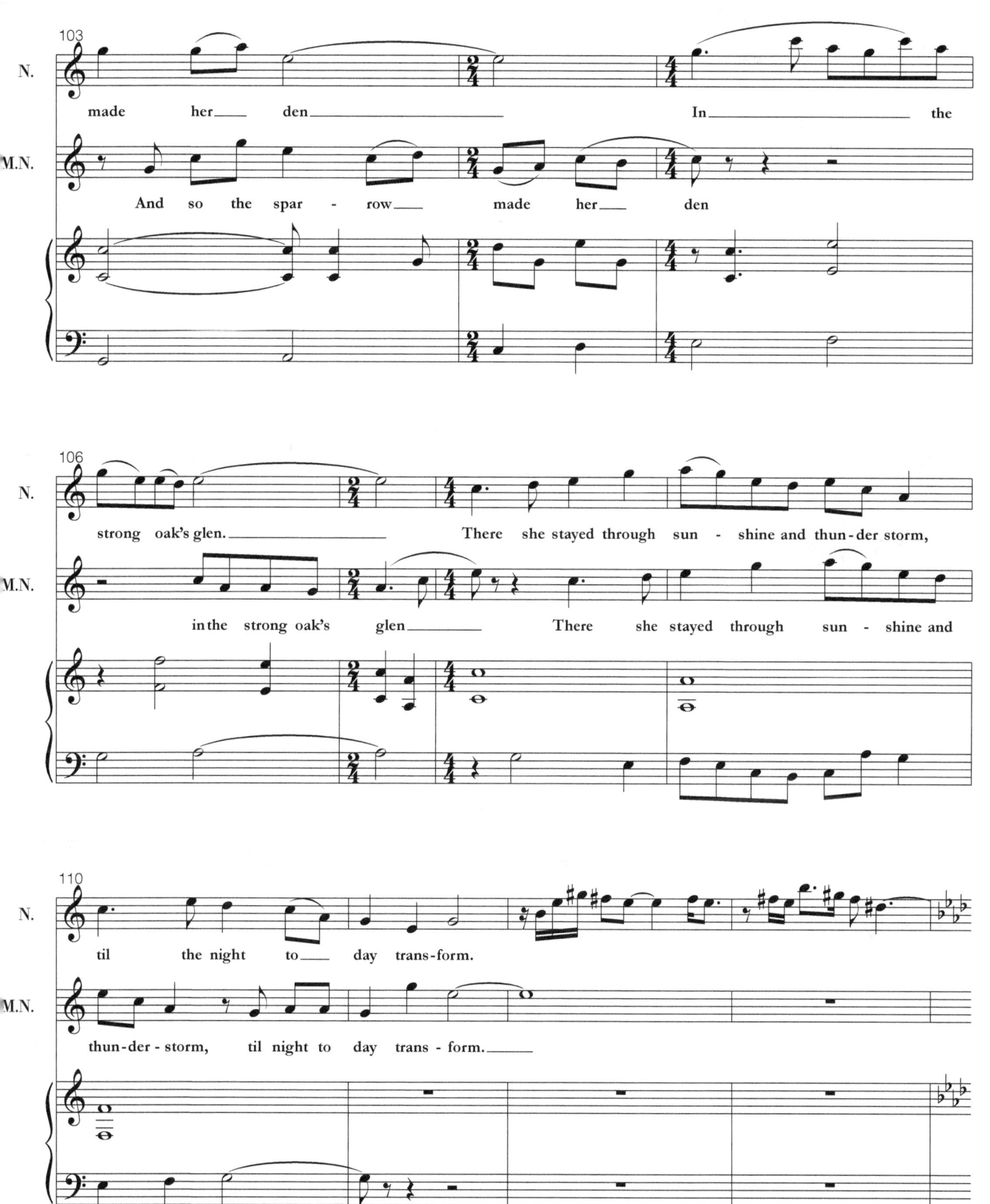

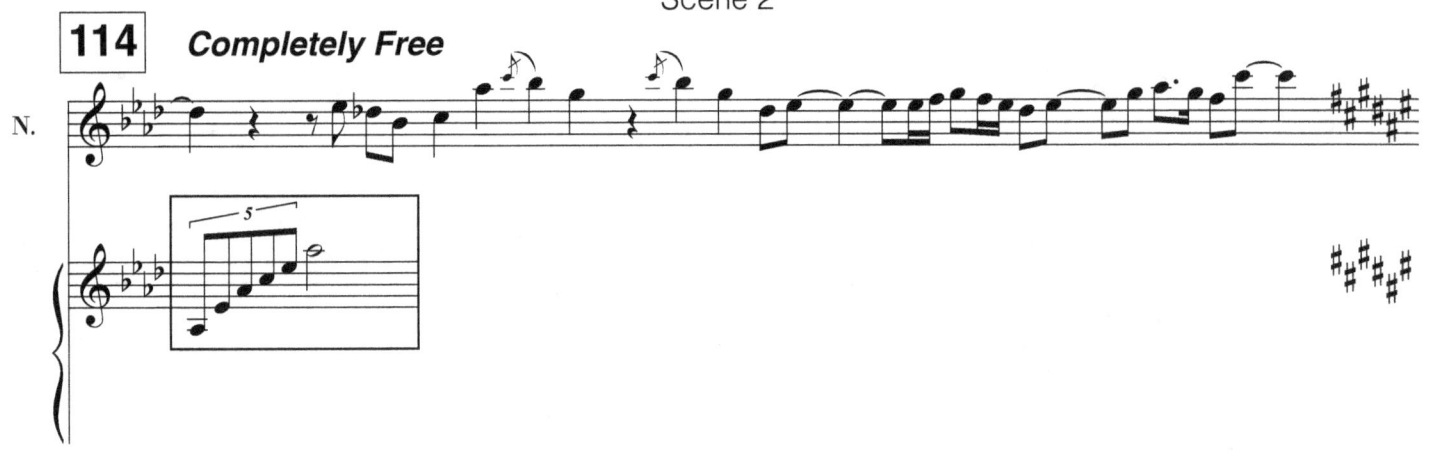

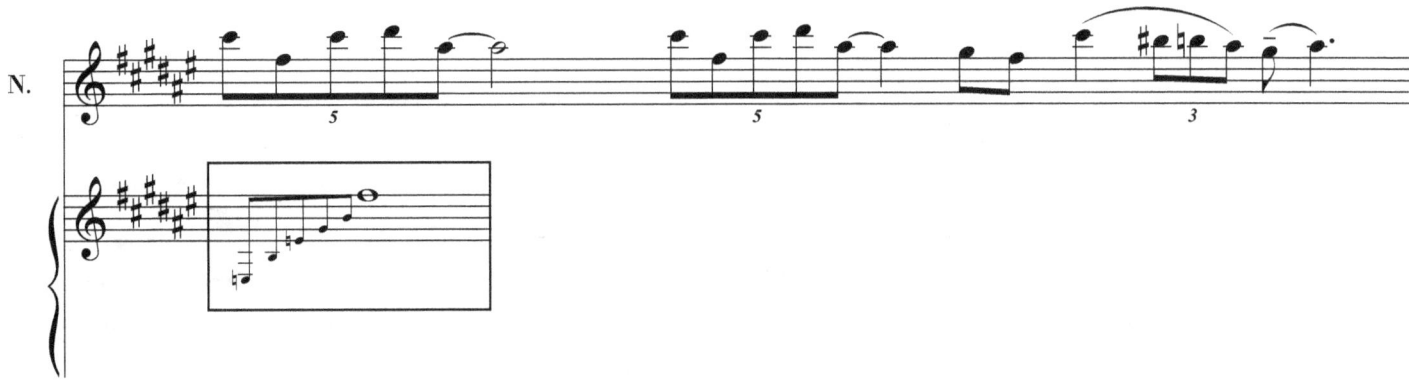

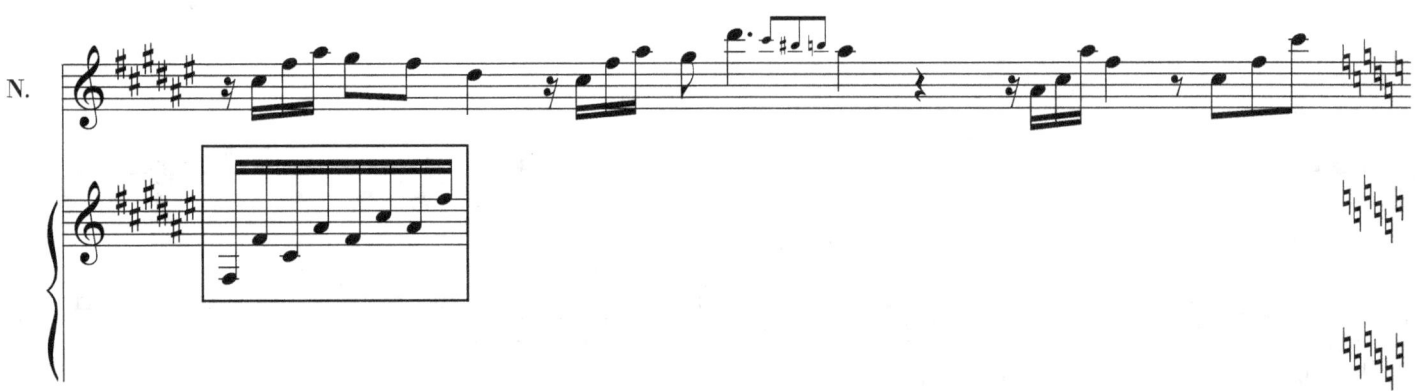

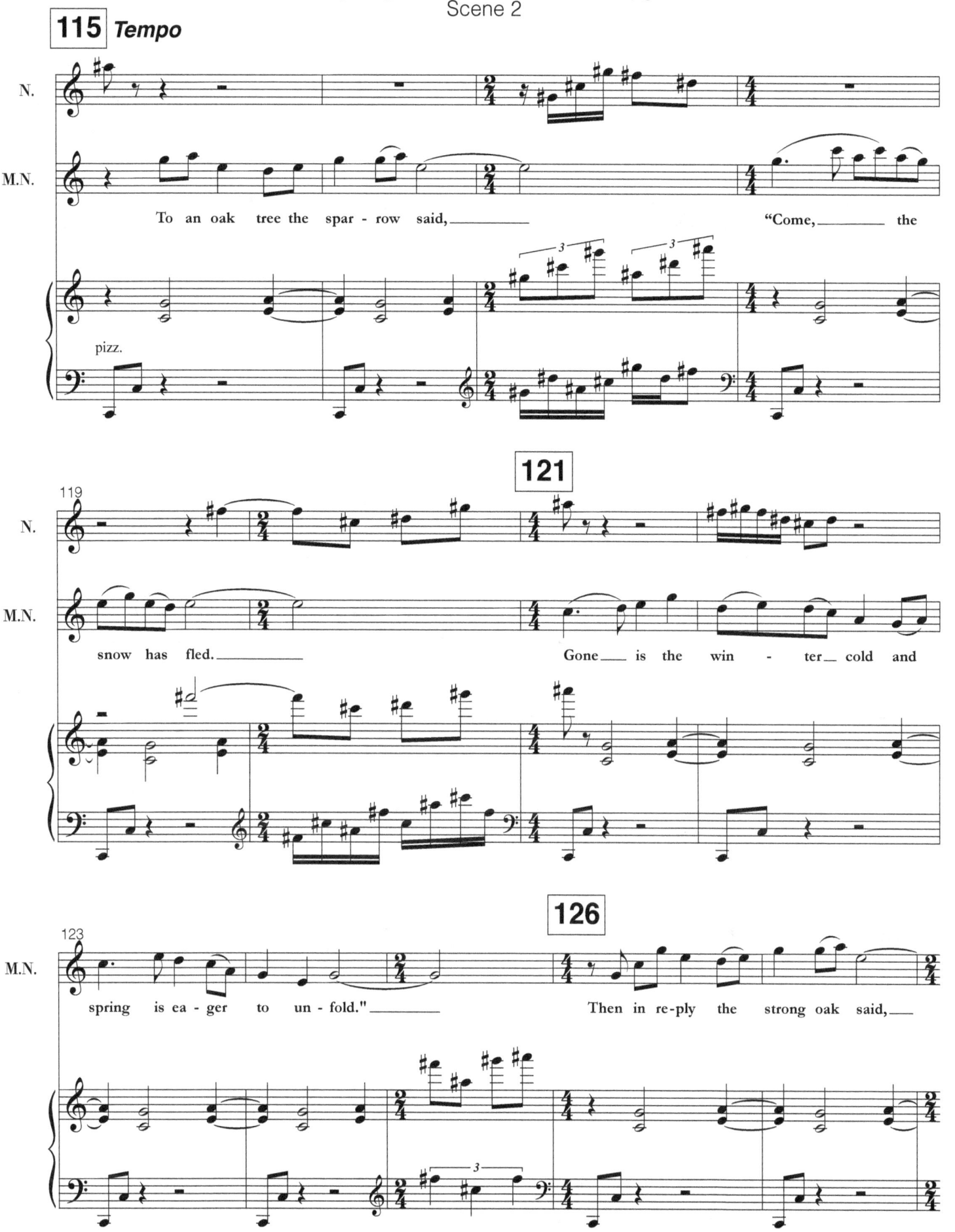

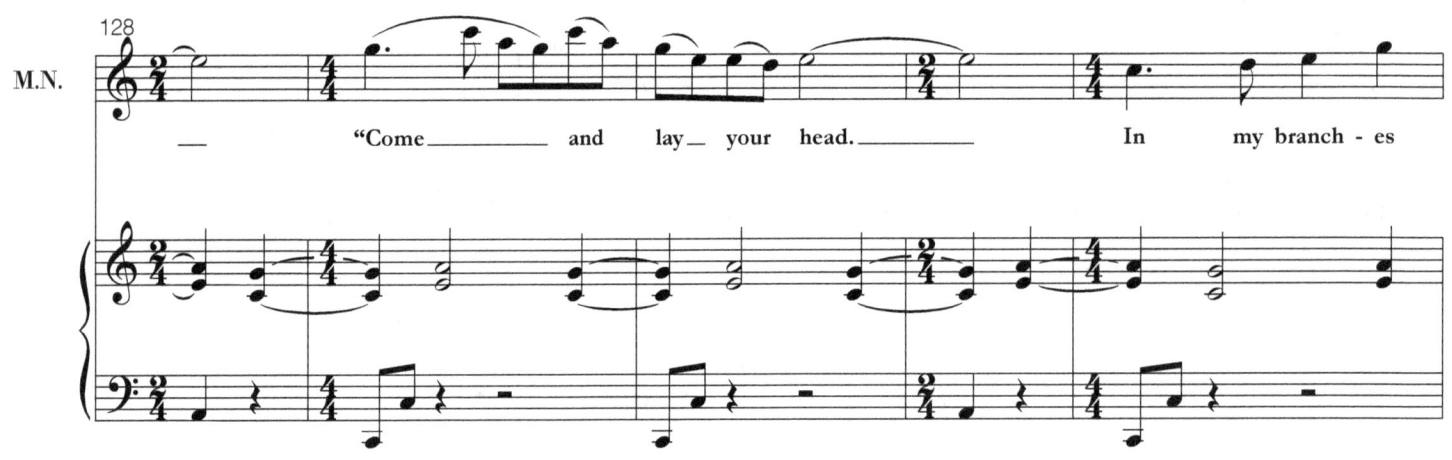

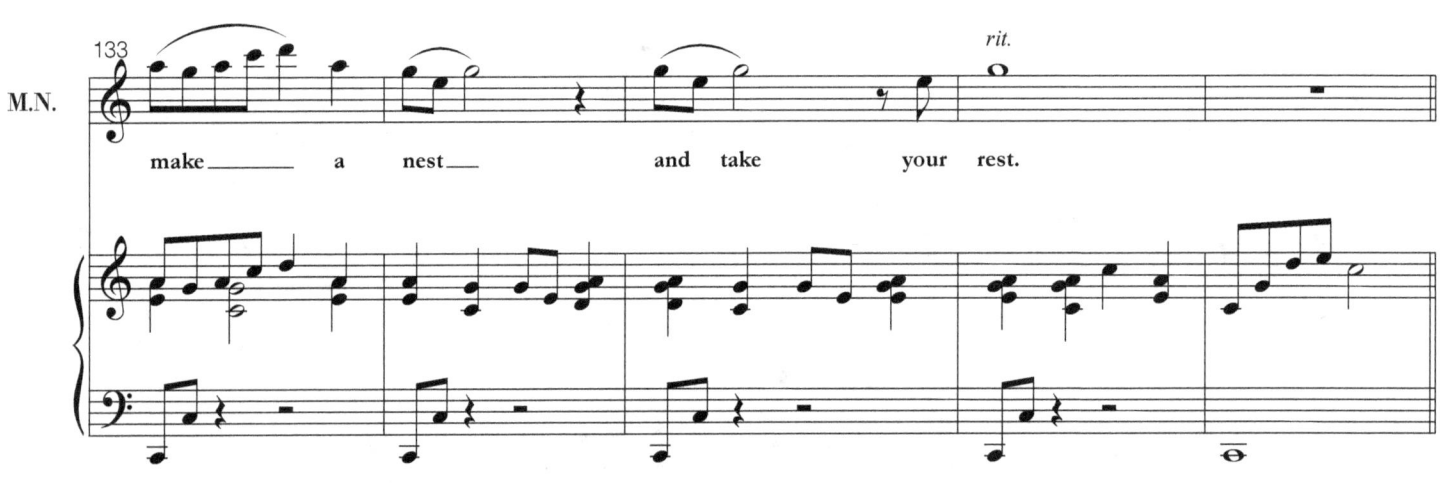

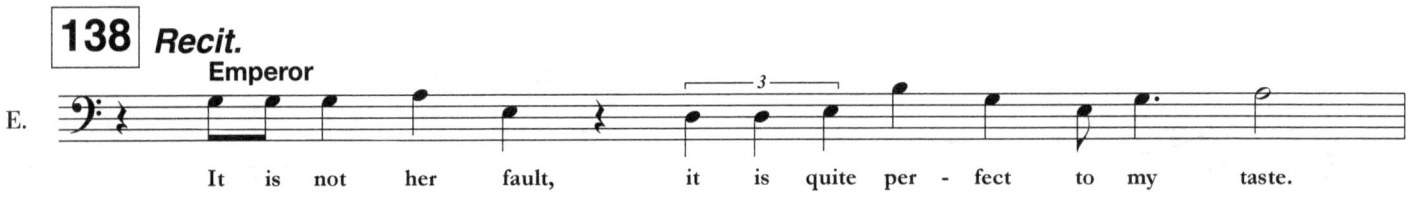

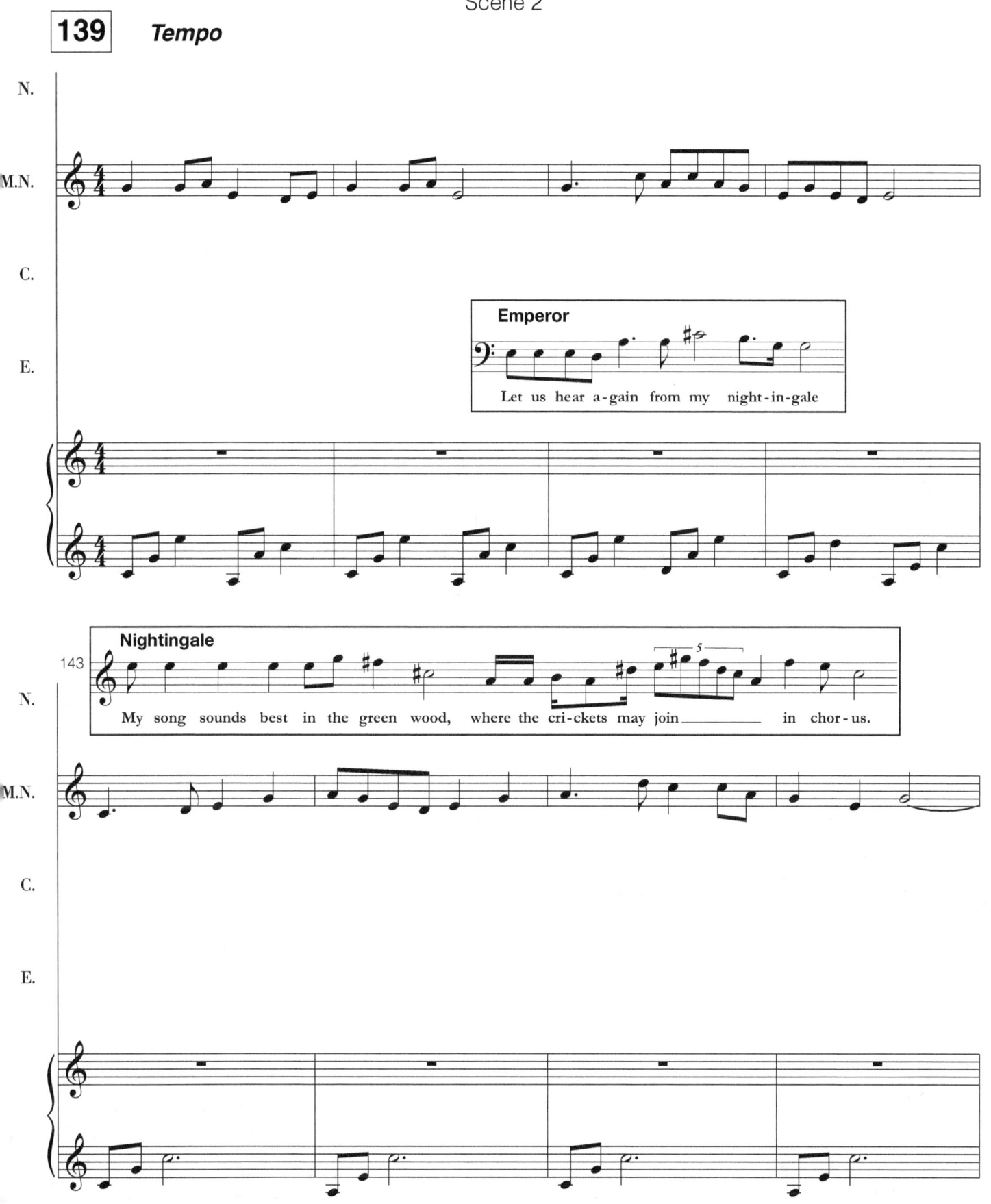

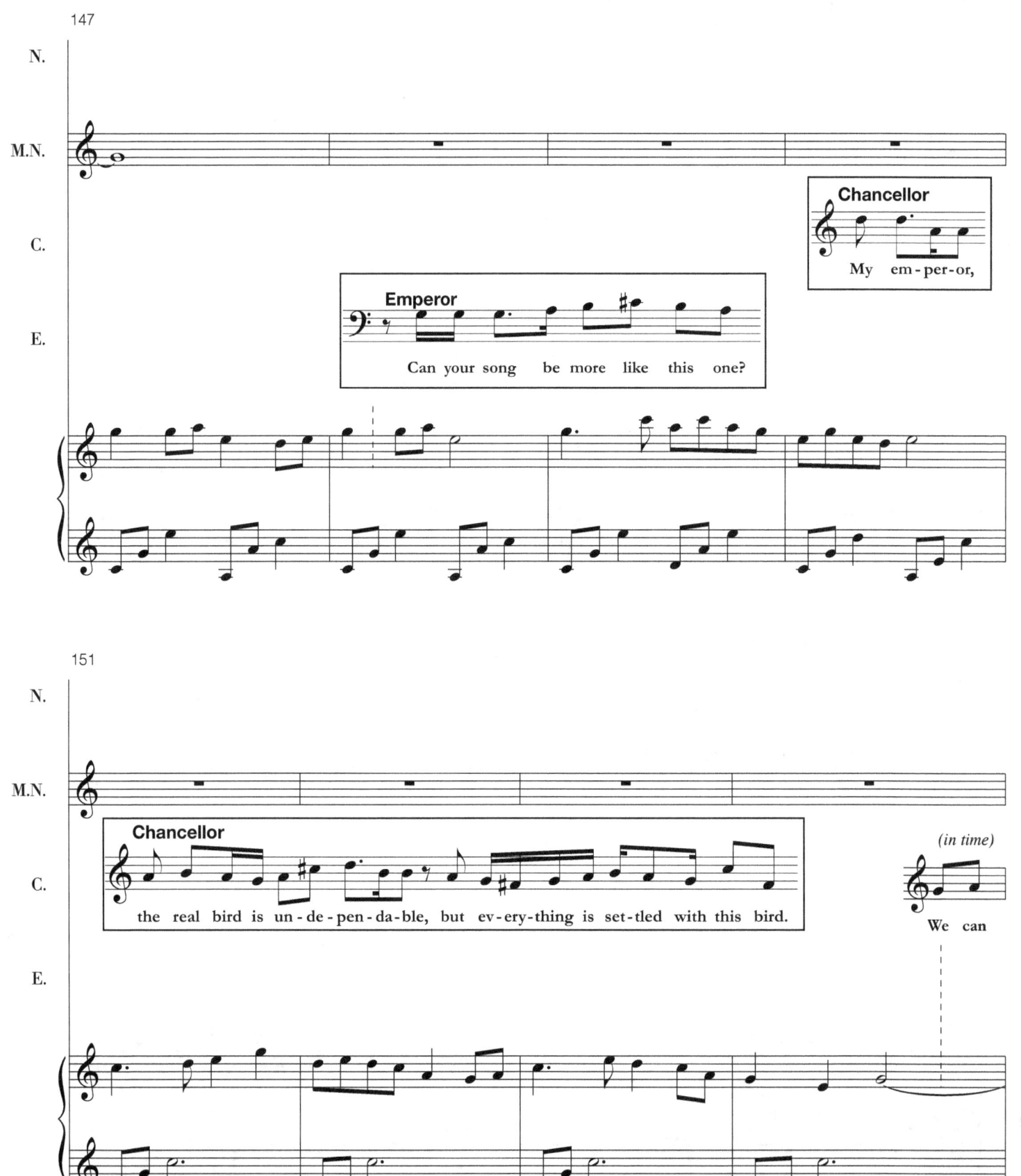

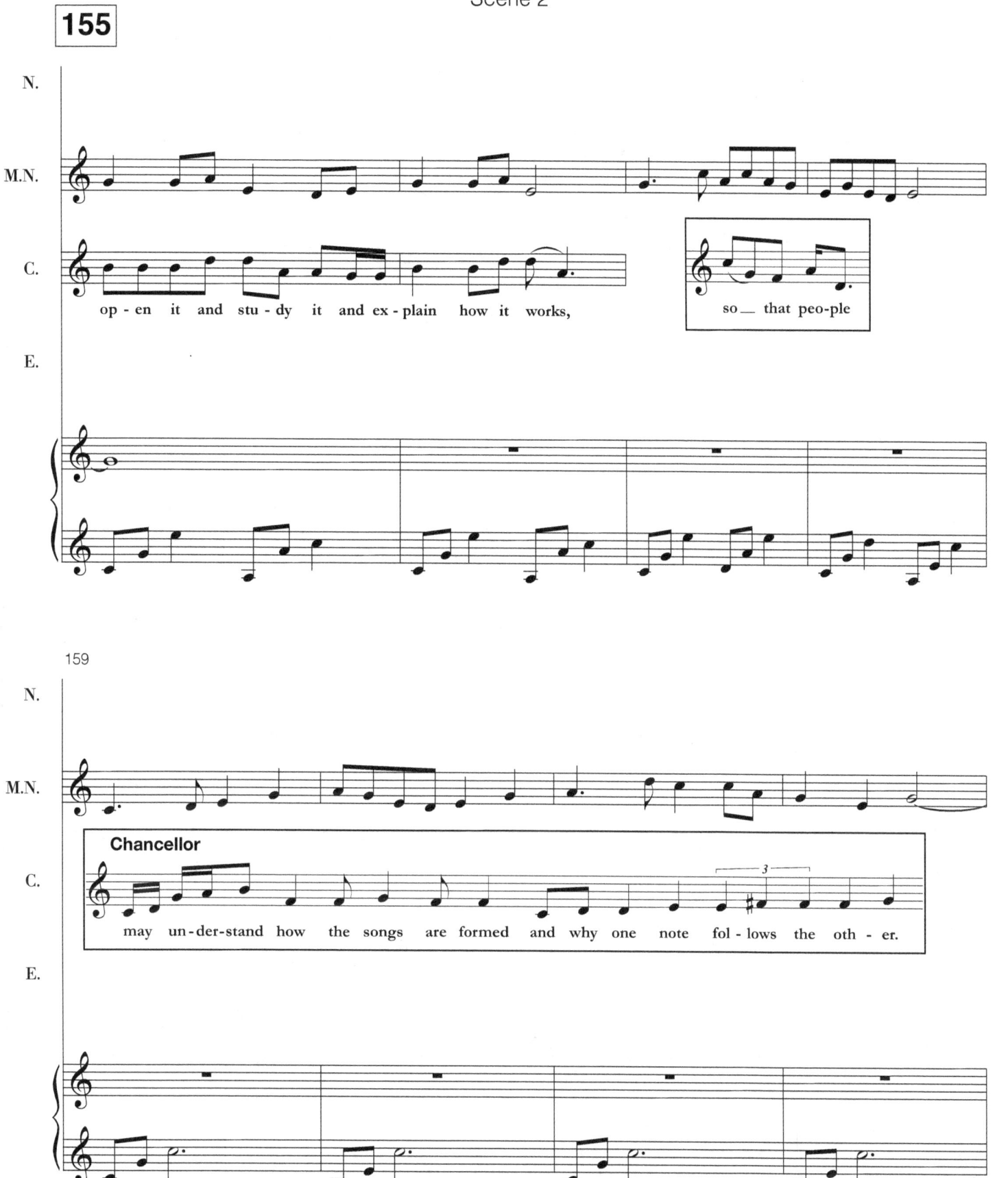

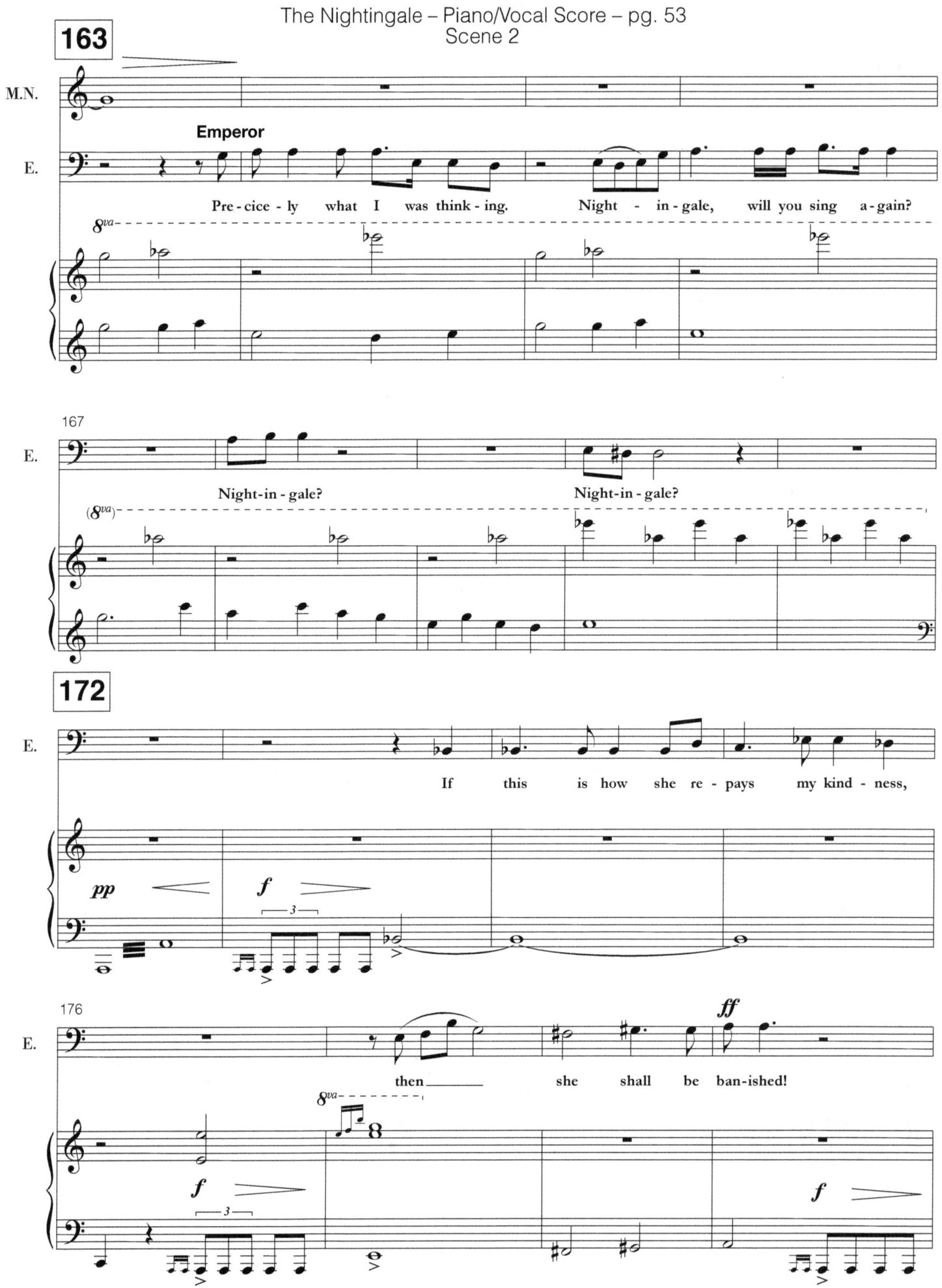

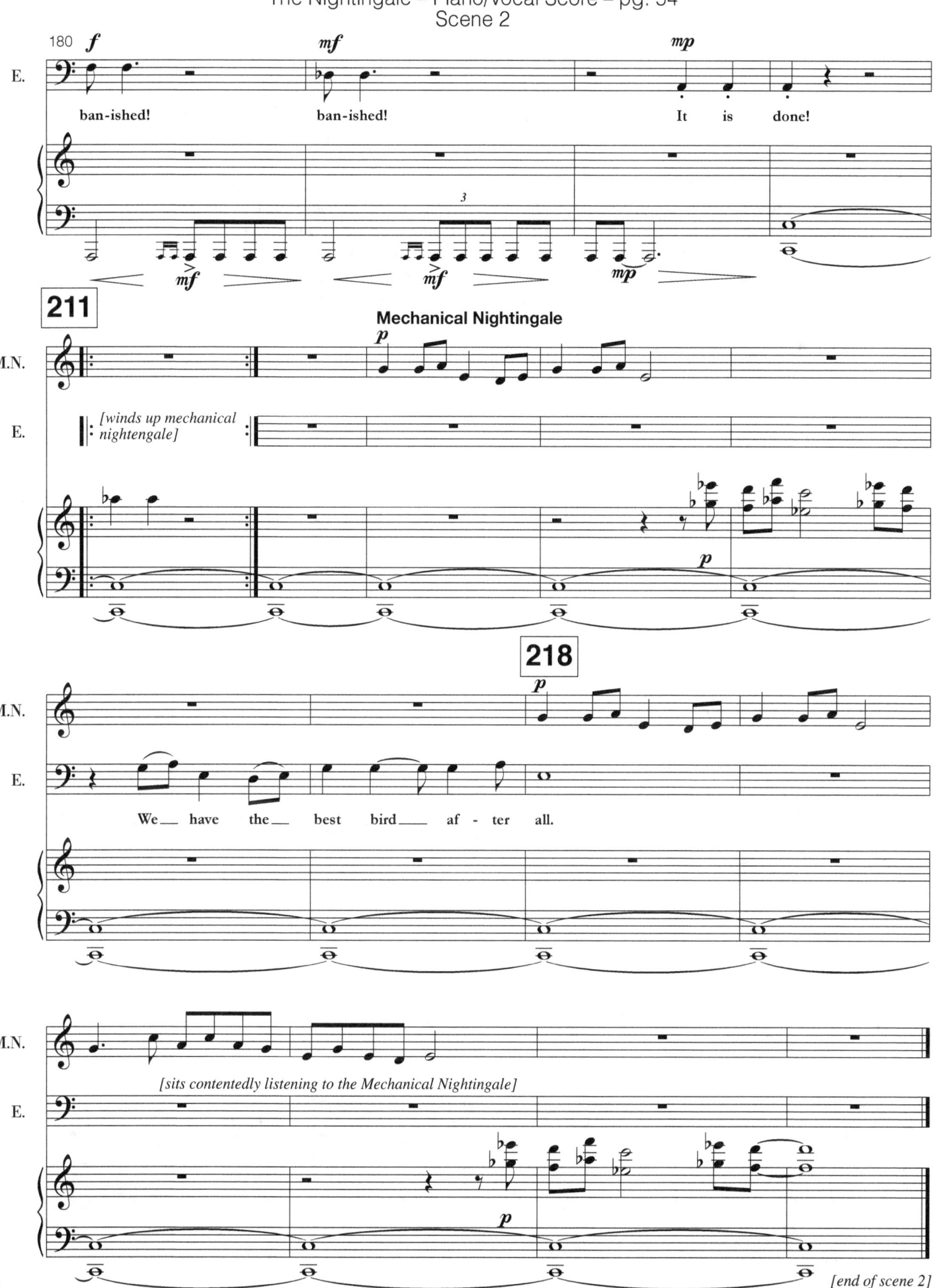

Scene 3

The Imperial Palace

Narrator, Death (Narrator), Spirit 1 (Kitchenmaid), Spirit 2 (Chancellor),
Emperor, Nightingale, Mechanical Nightingale (mute)

The emperor lays sick in bed. In the room are a crown, a sword, and an imperial banner.
The Narrator, as he is singing about the sing, should actually take on the persona of Death,
placing a large black cloak over his head, or around his neck. The two spirits (previously
the Kitchenmaid and the Chancellor) should be outfitted with an easily removable pale
shawl that should seem bery ghost-like. This way, if they are included in the staging of the final
moments of this scene, they may easily get back into their other costumes.

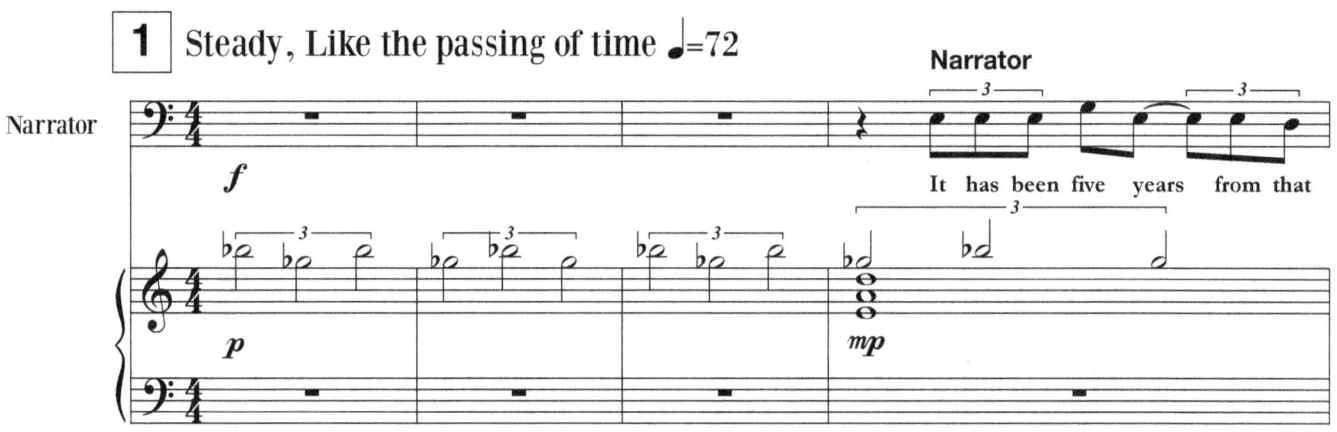

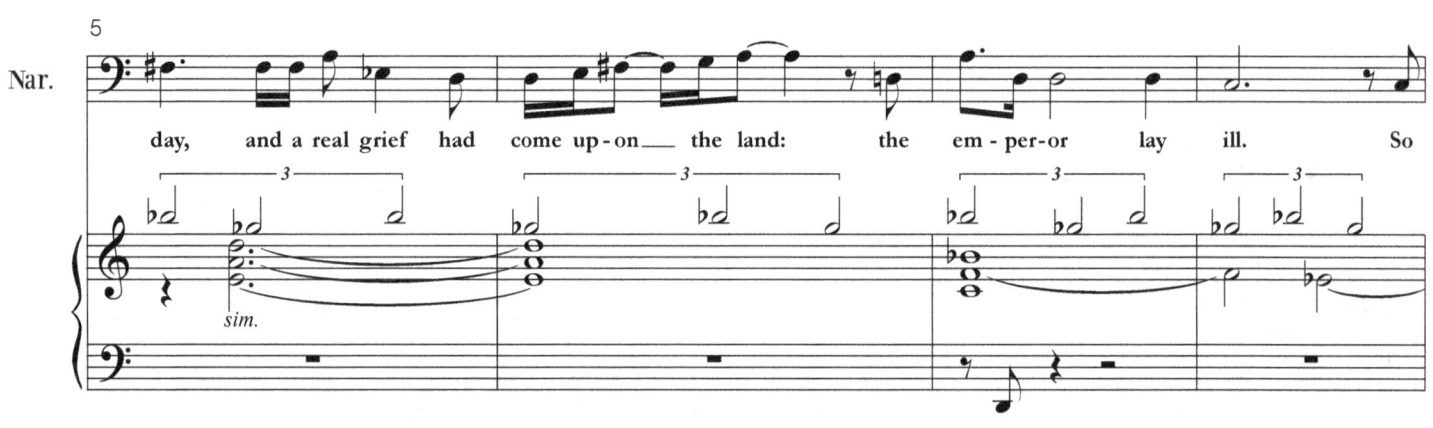

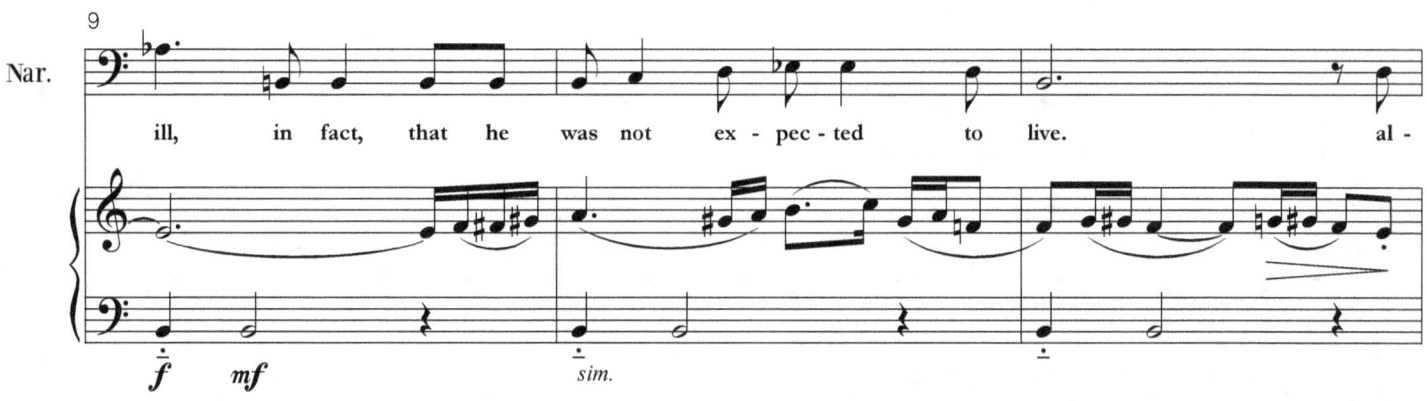

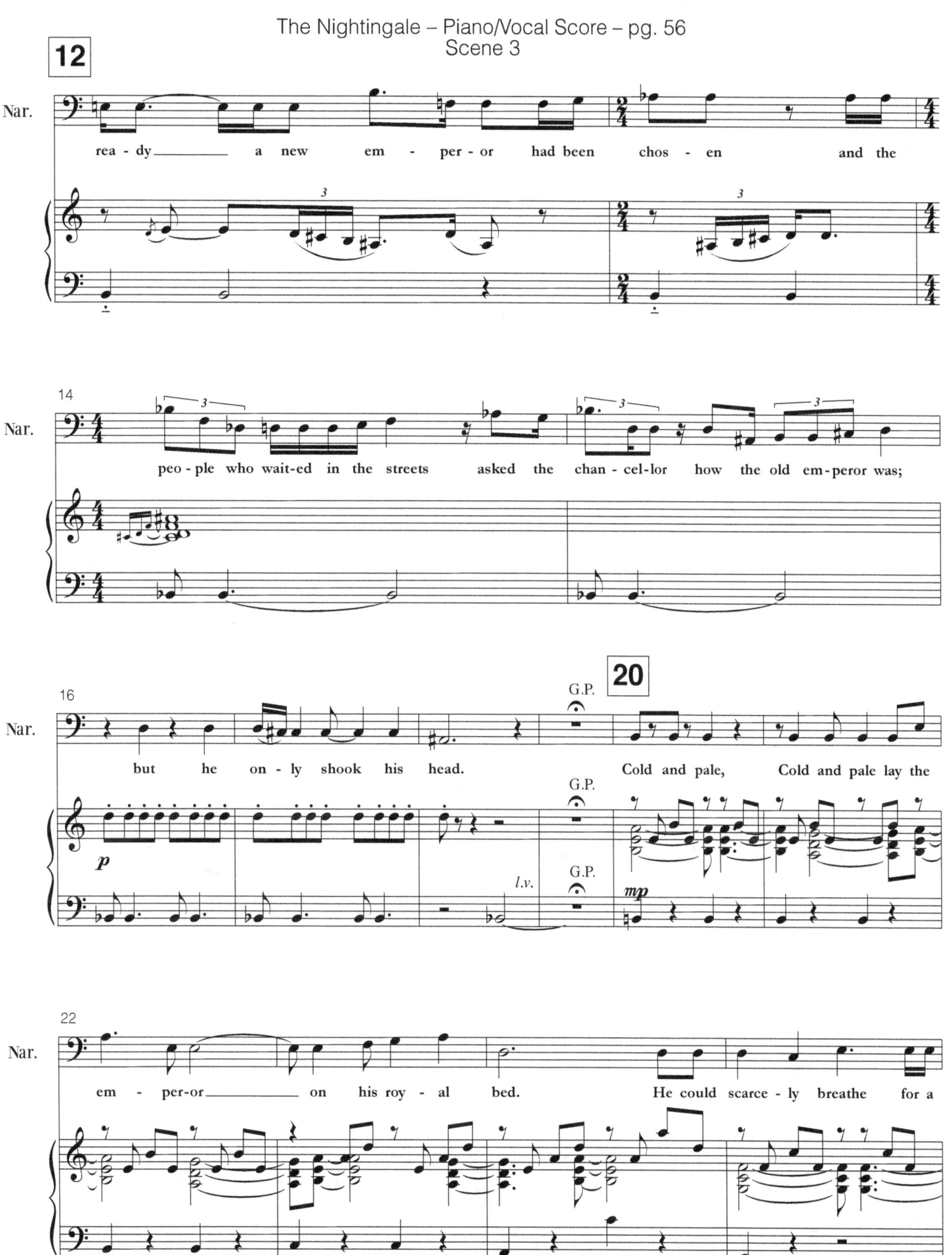

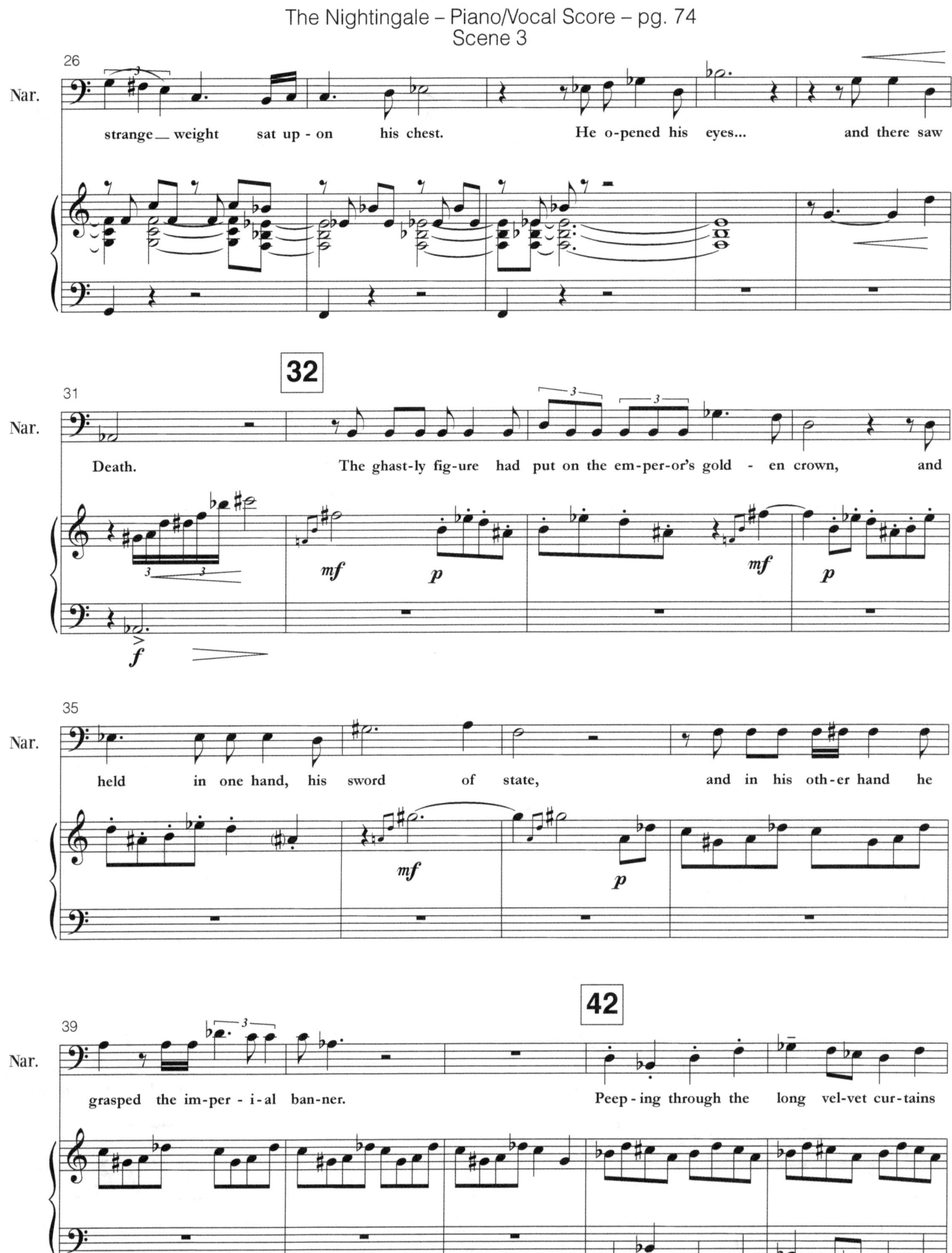

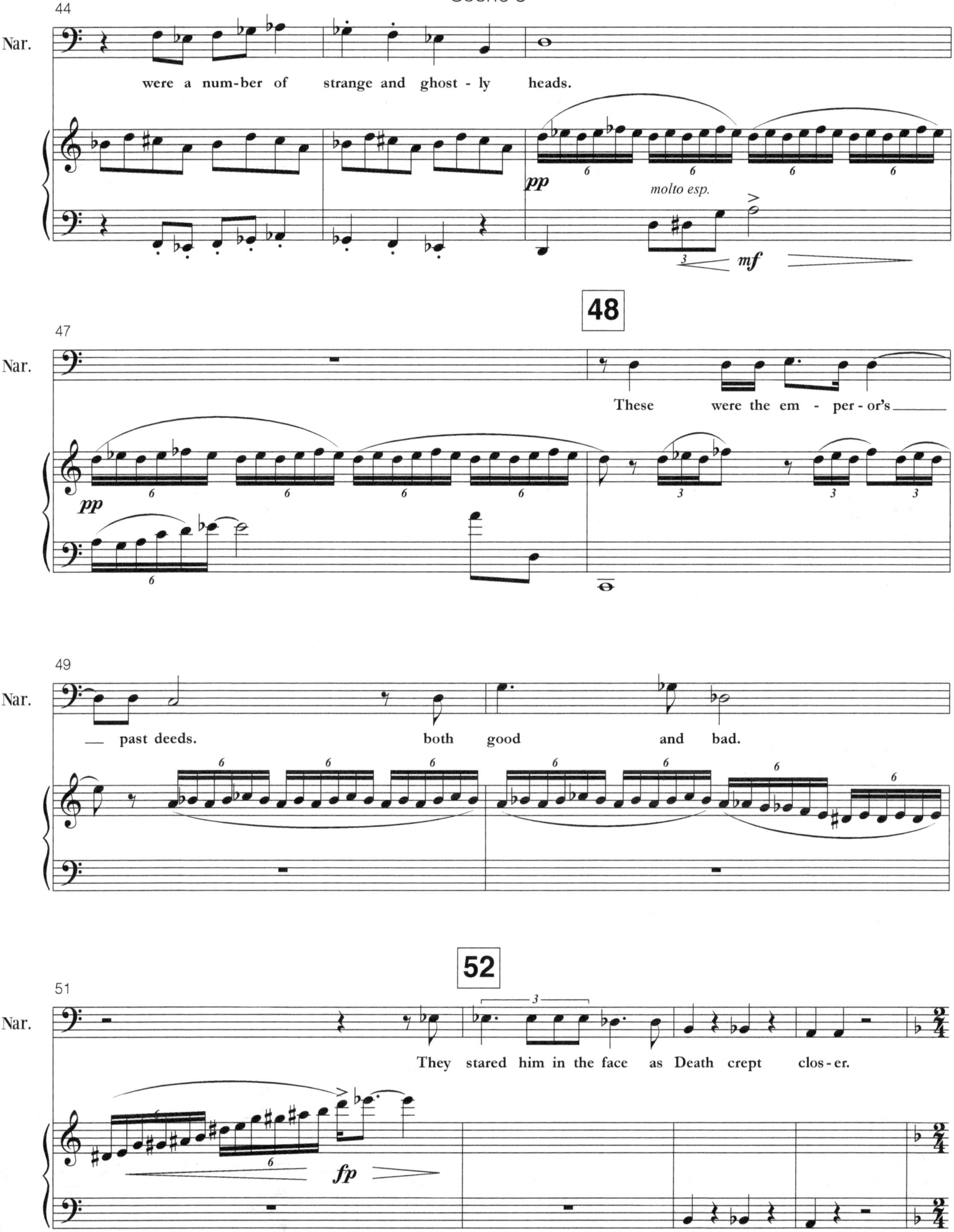
44
Nar.
were a num-ber of strange and ghost - ly heads.
pp
molto esp.
mf
47
48
These were the em - per - or's
pp
49
past deeds. both good and bad.
51
52
They stared him in the face as Death crept clos - er.
fp

Scene 3

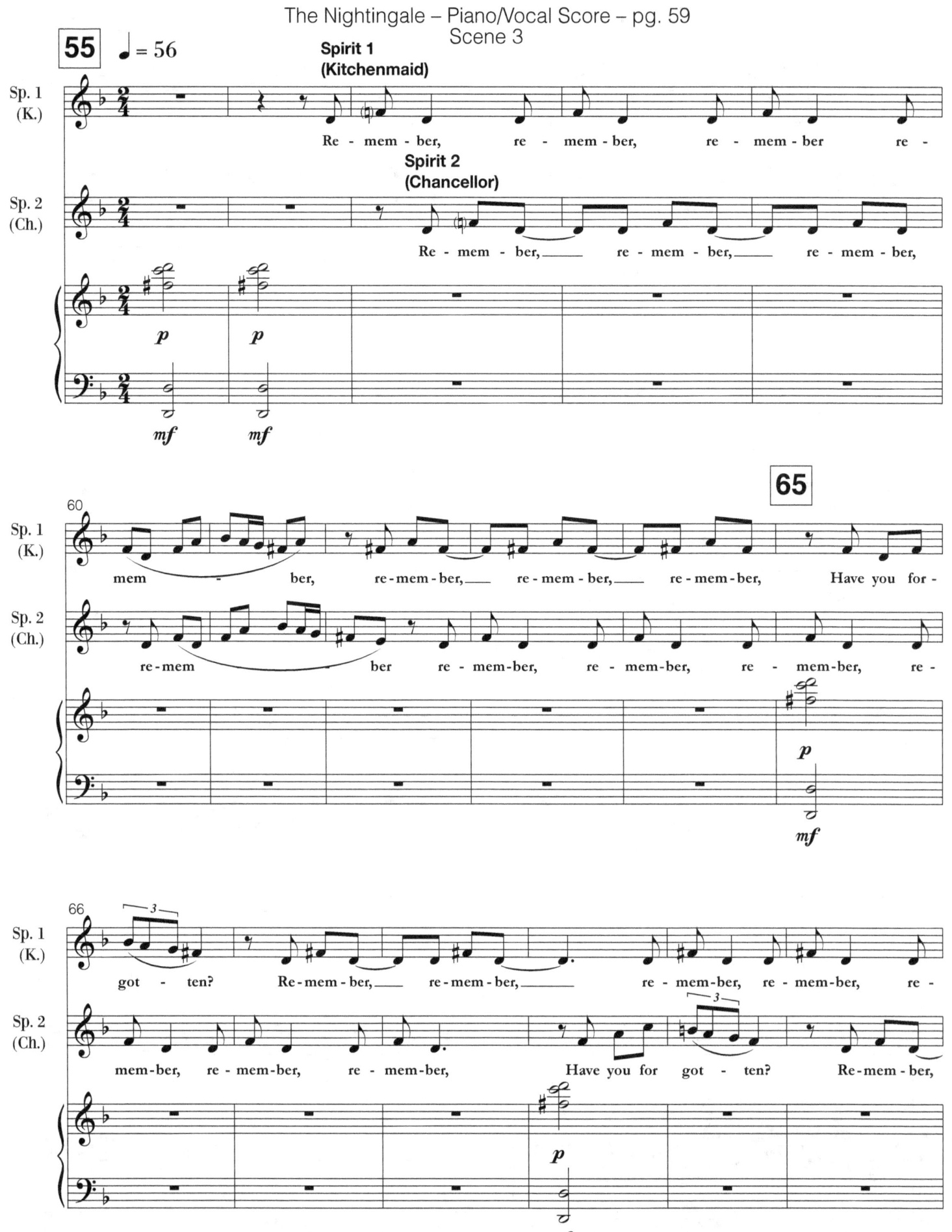

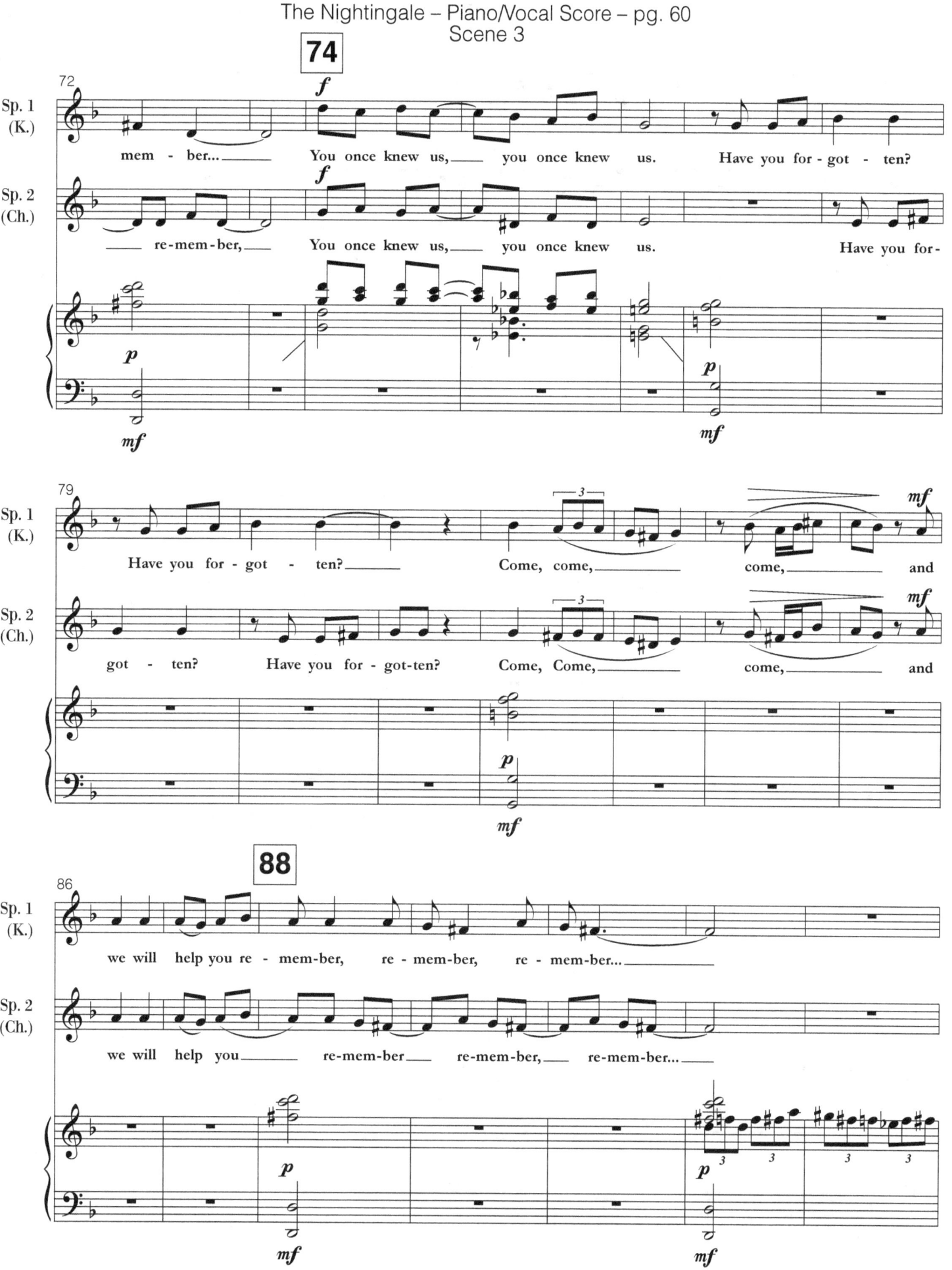

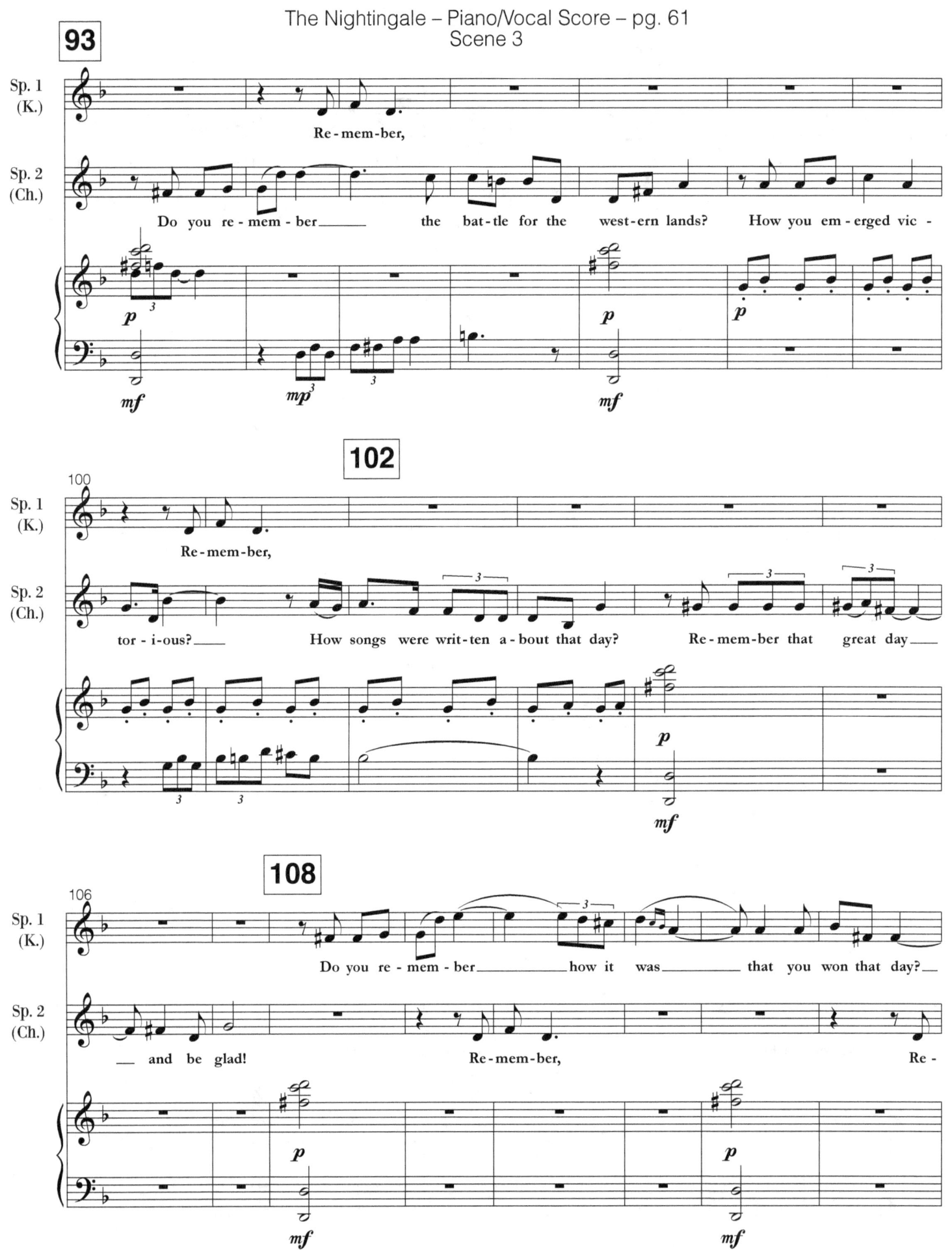

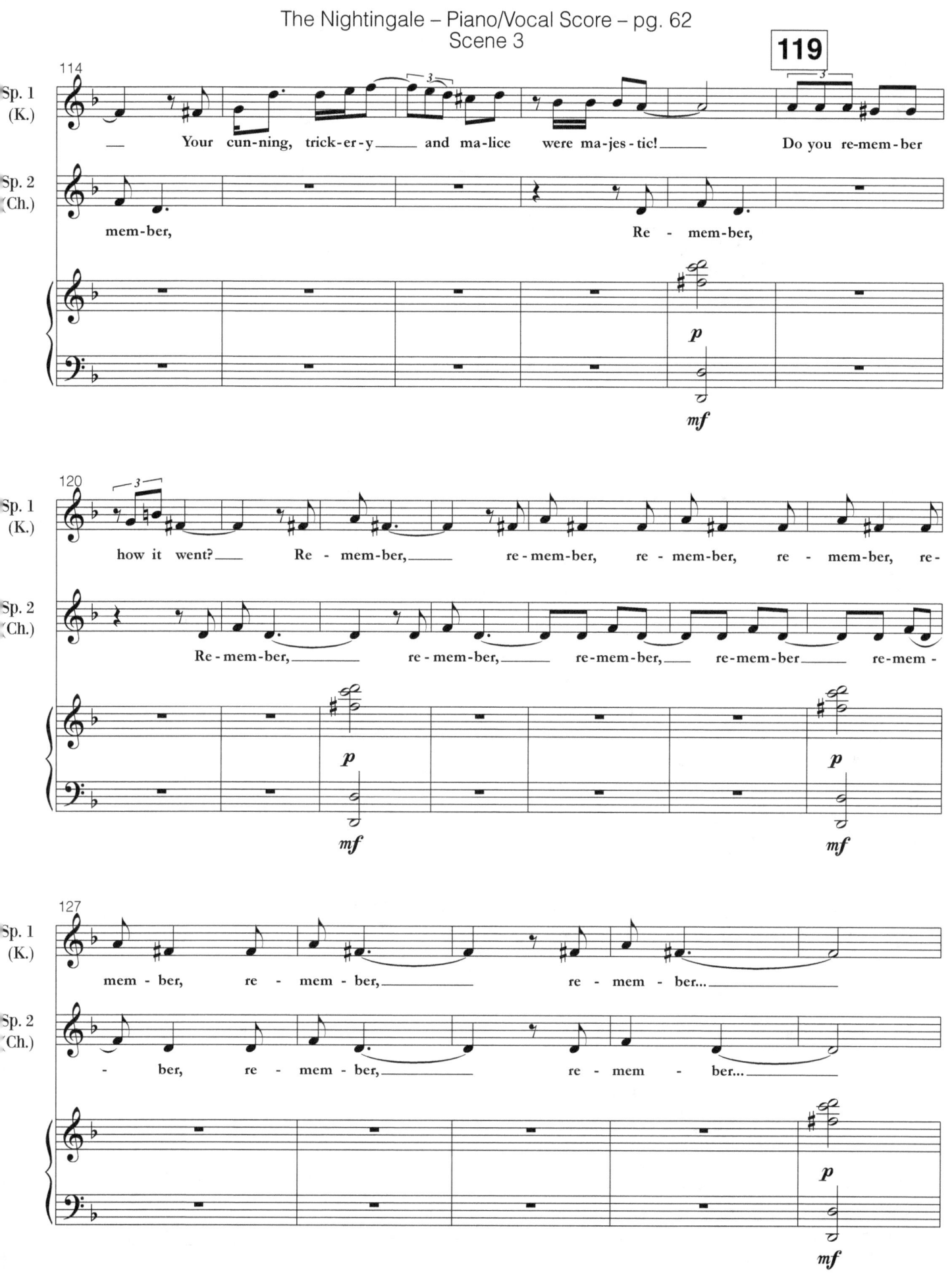

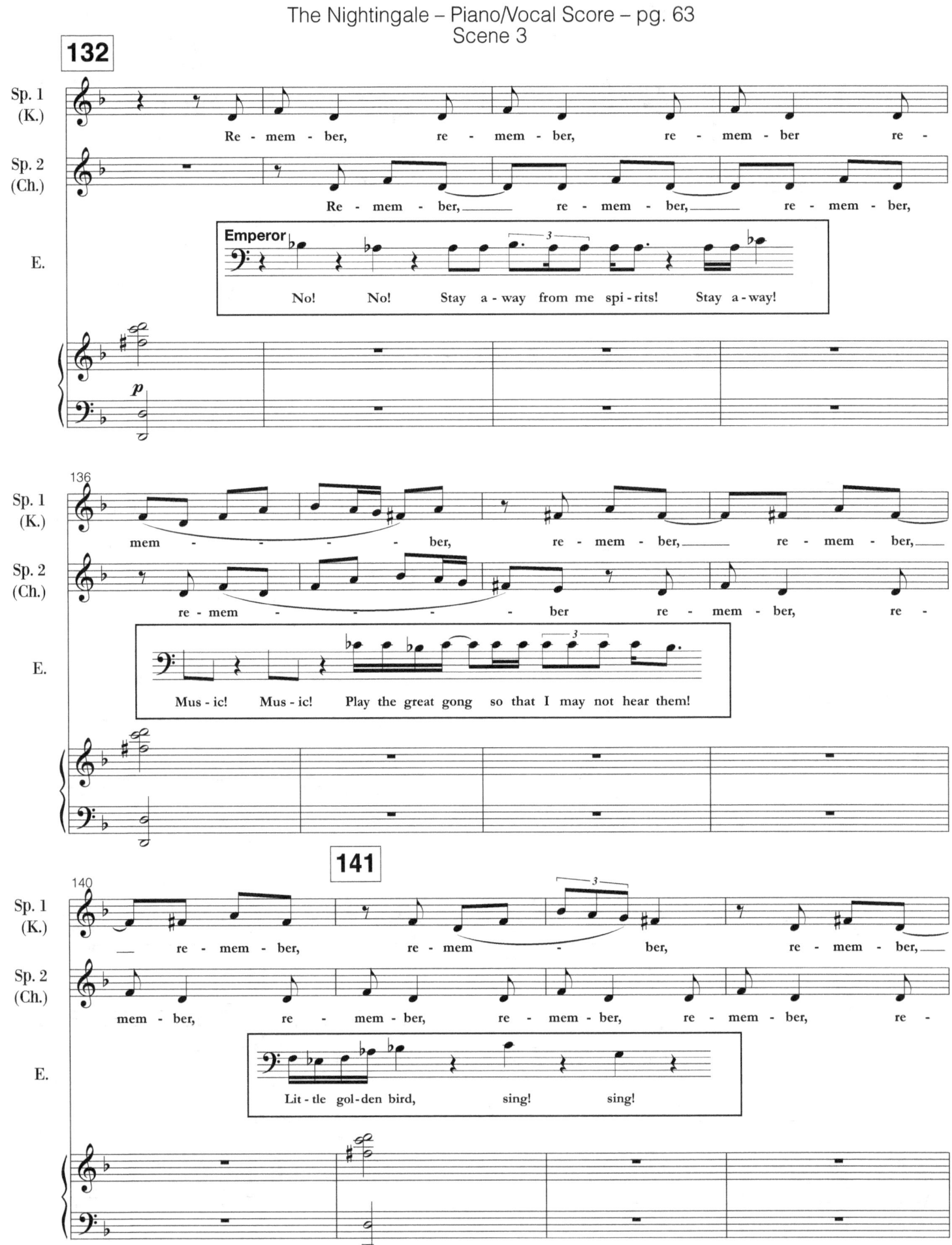

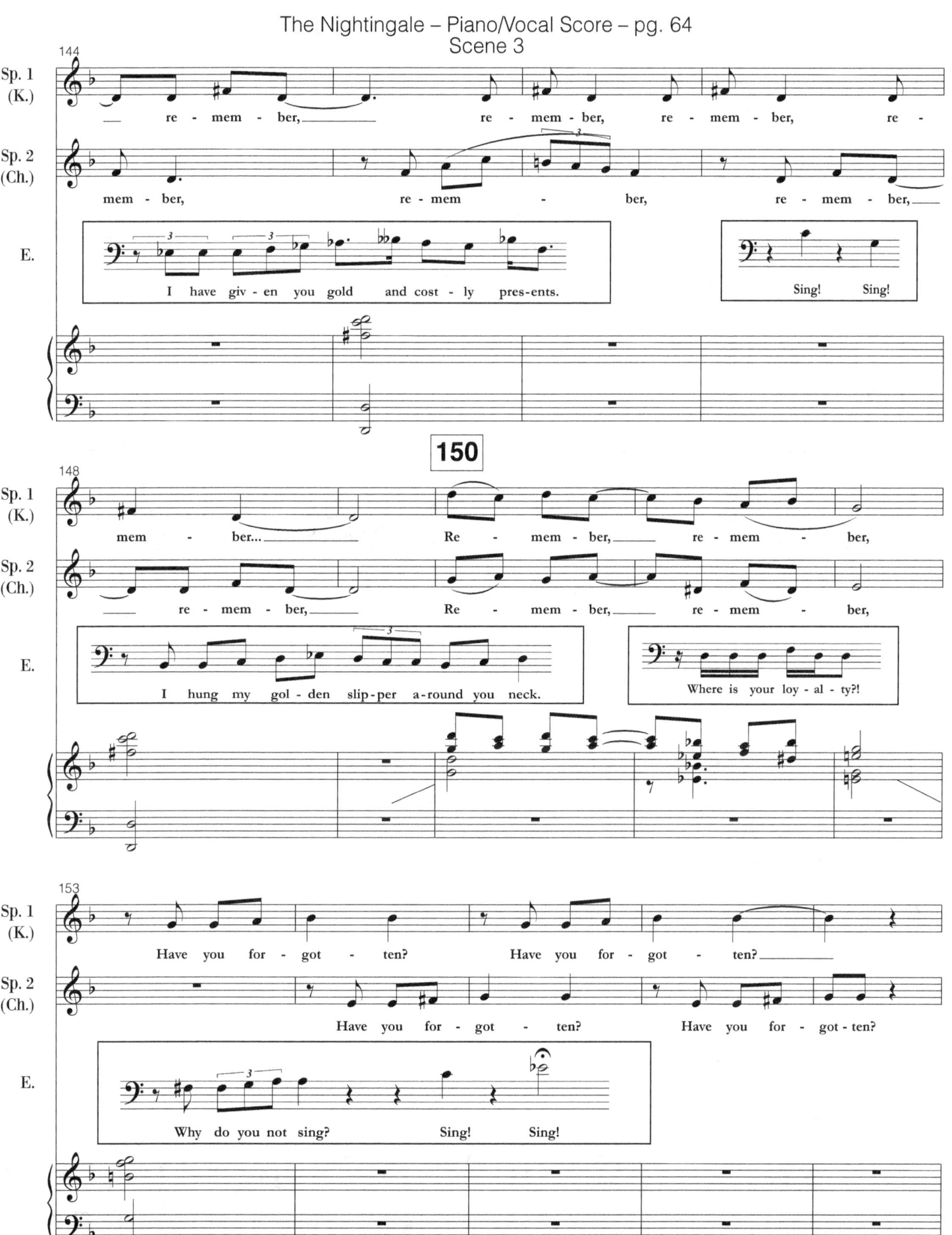

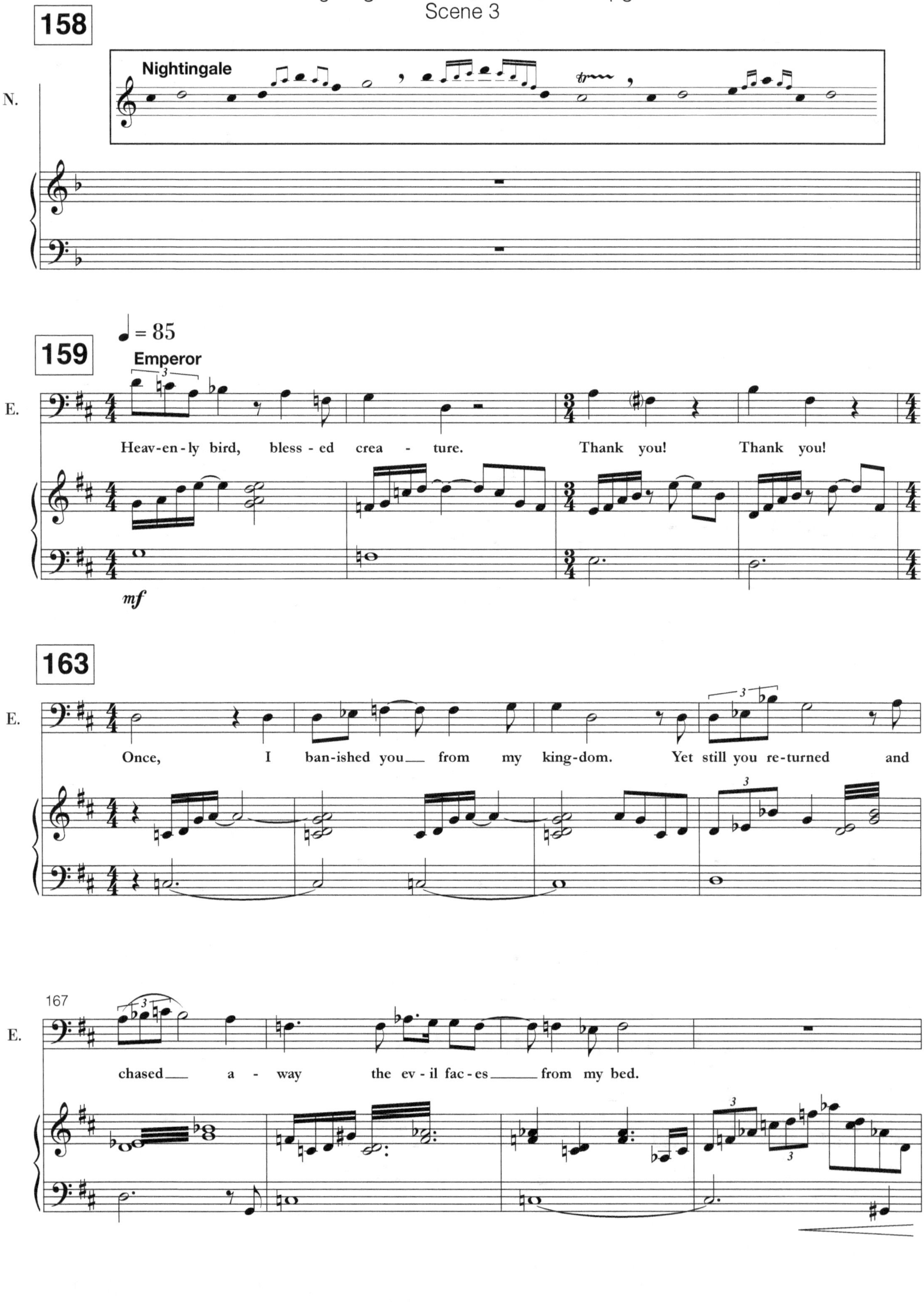

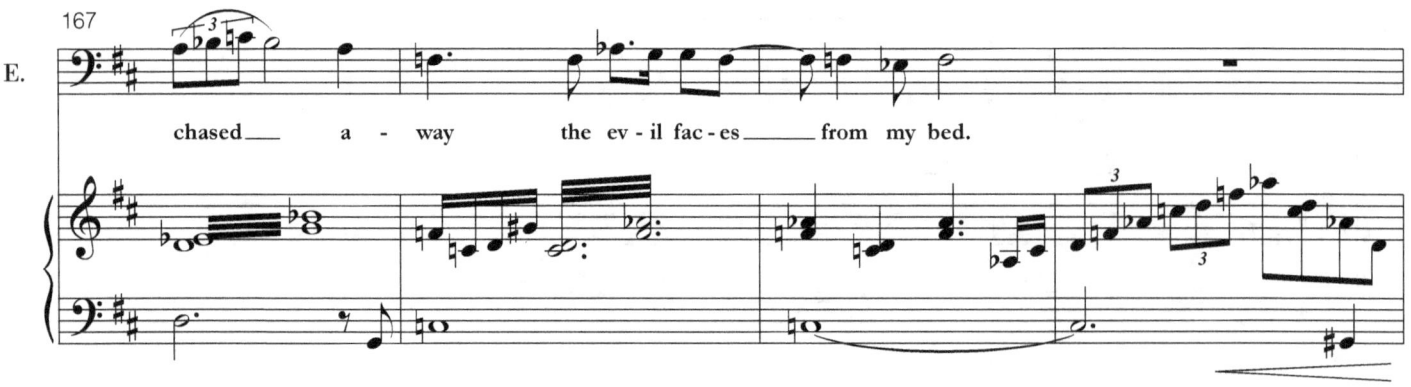

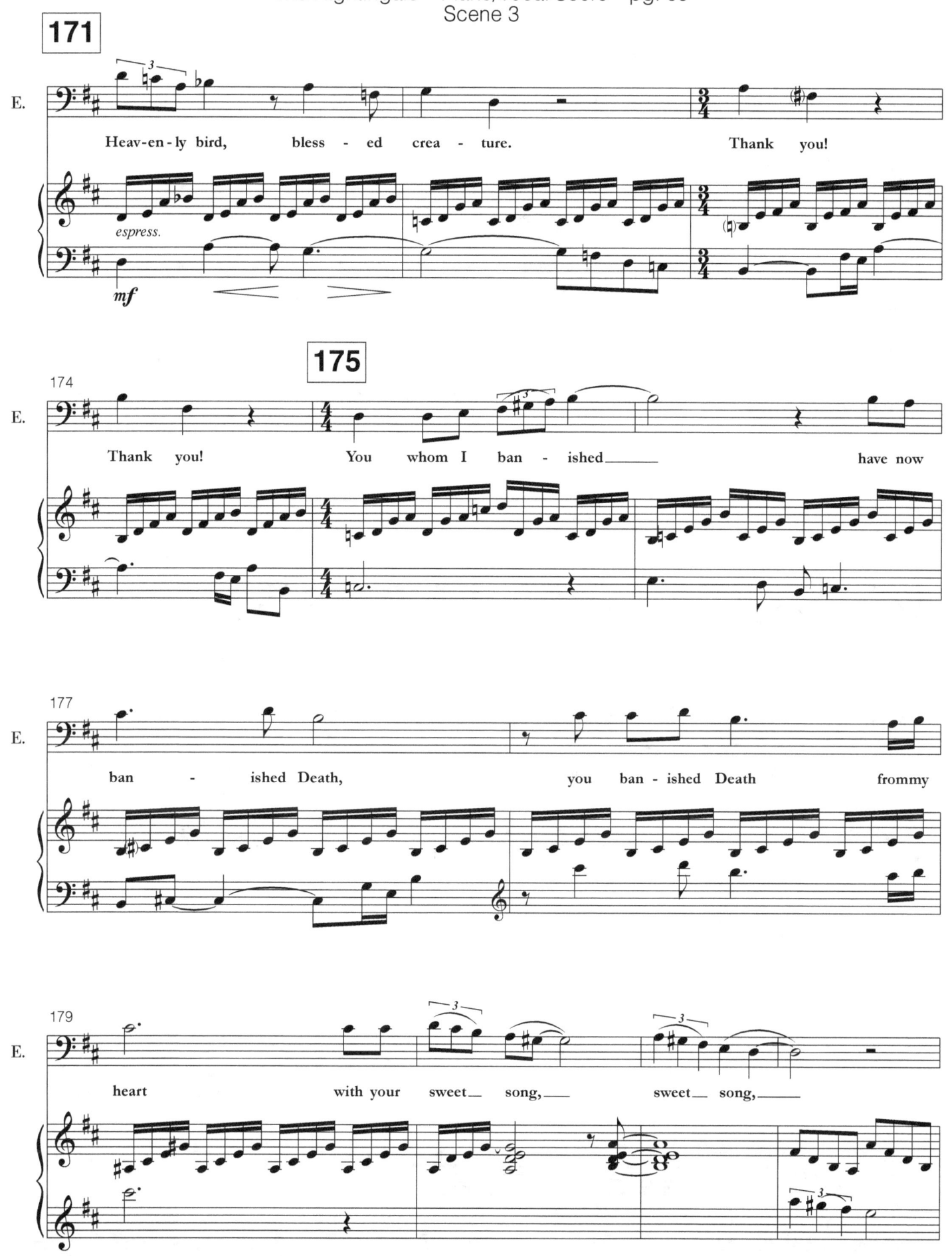

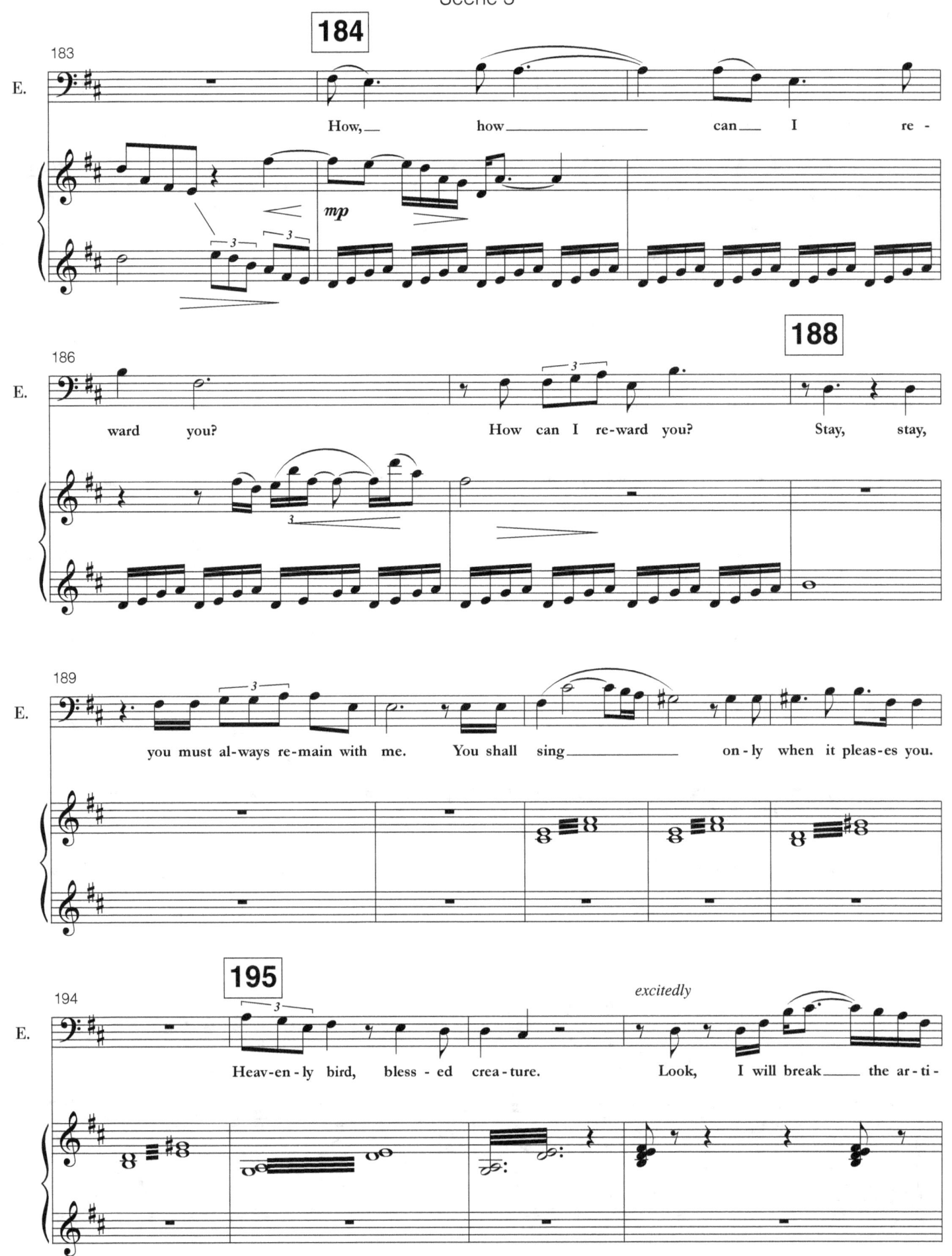

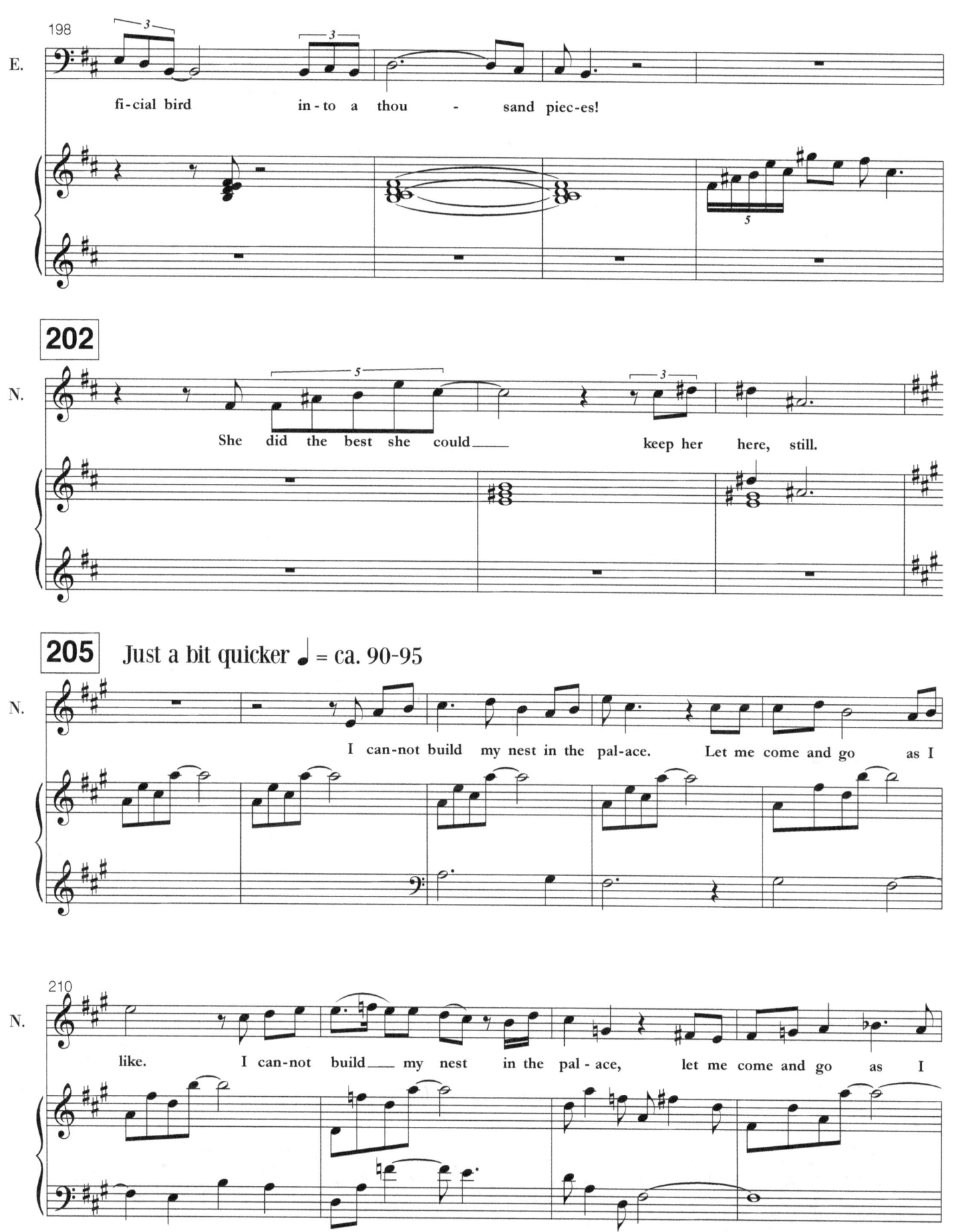

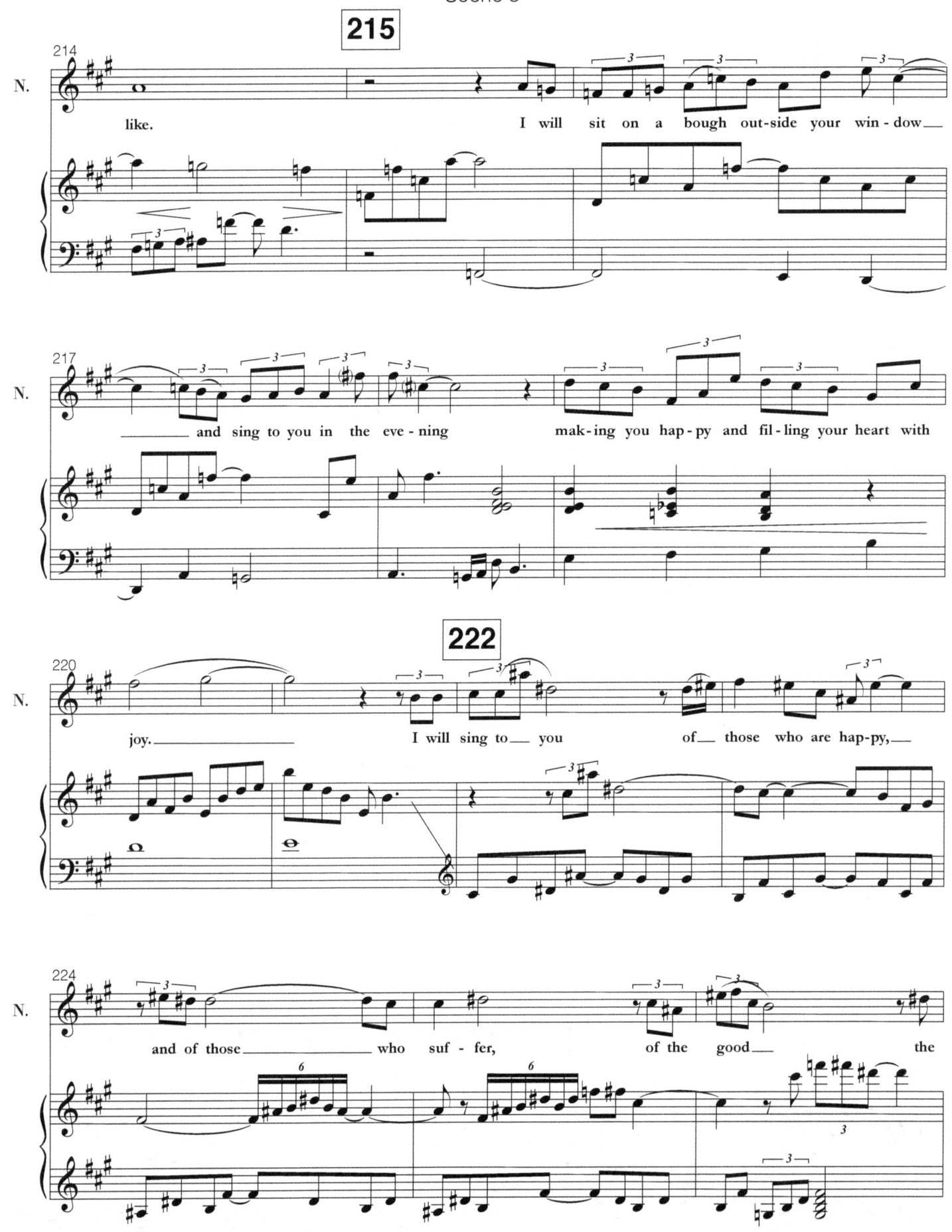

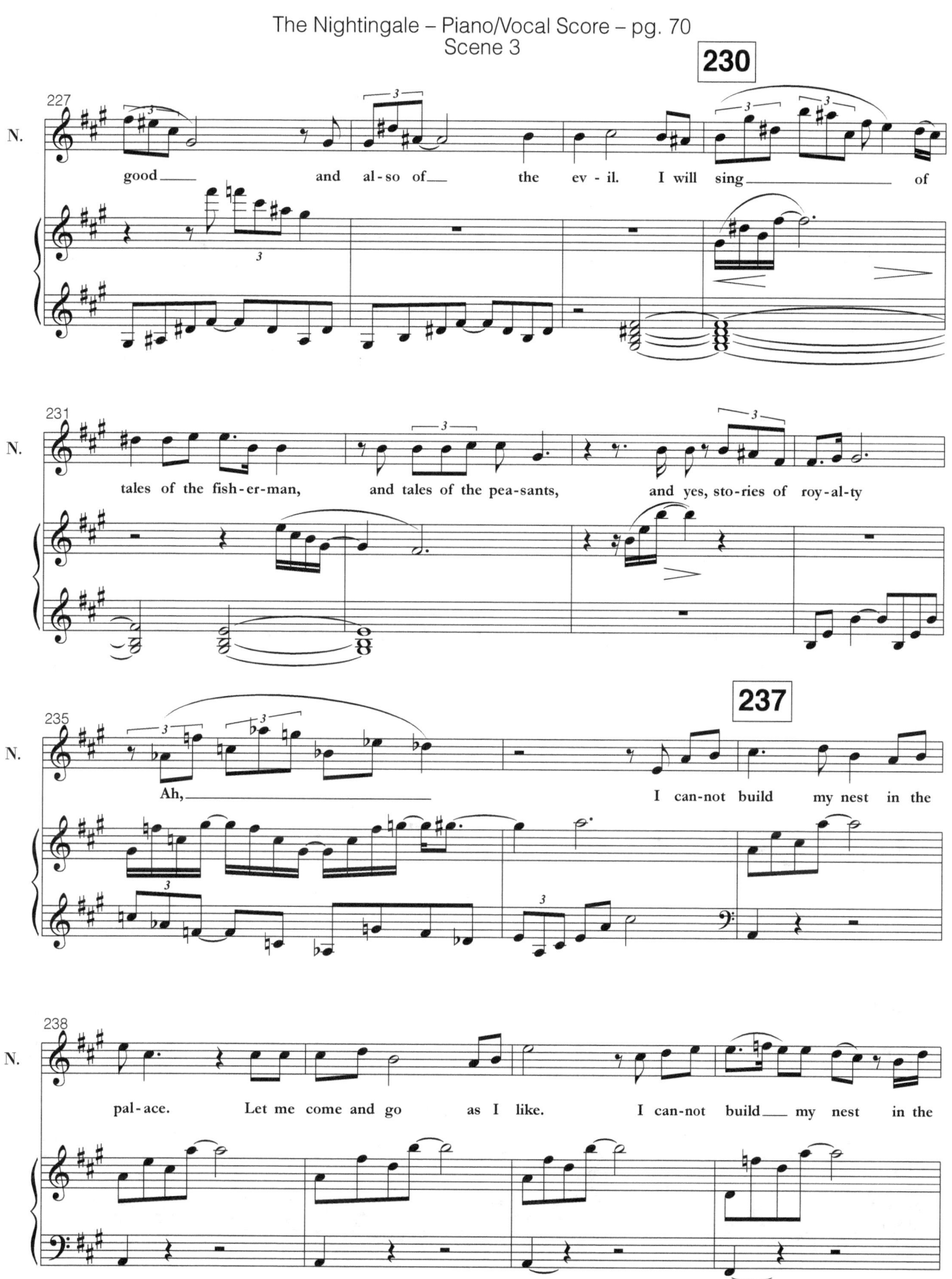

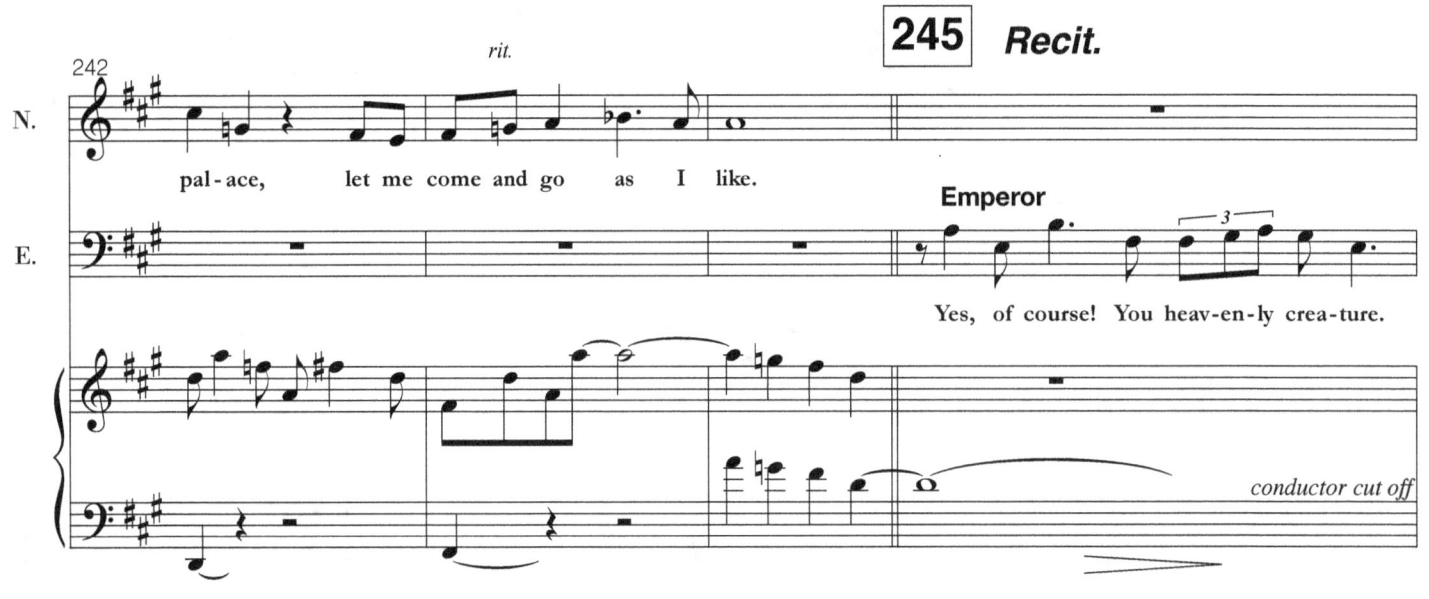

245 *Recit.*

Emperor

N. pal-ace, let me come and go as I like.

E. Yes, of course! You heav-en-ly crea-ture.

conductor cut off

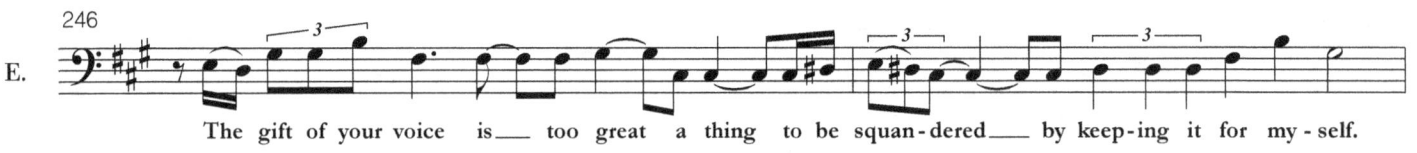

E. The gift of your voice is— too great a thing to be squan-dered— by keep-ing it for my-self.

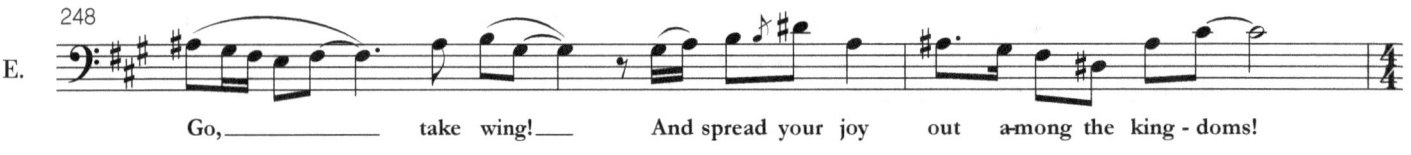

E. Go,——— take wing!— And spread your joy out a-mong the king-doms!

250 ♩ = 85

Narrator

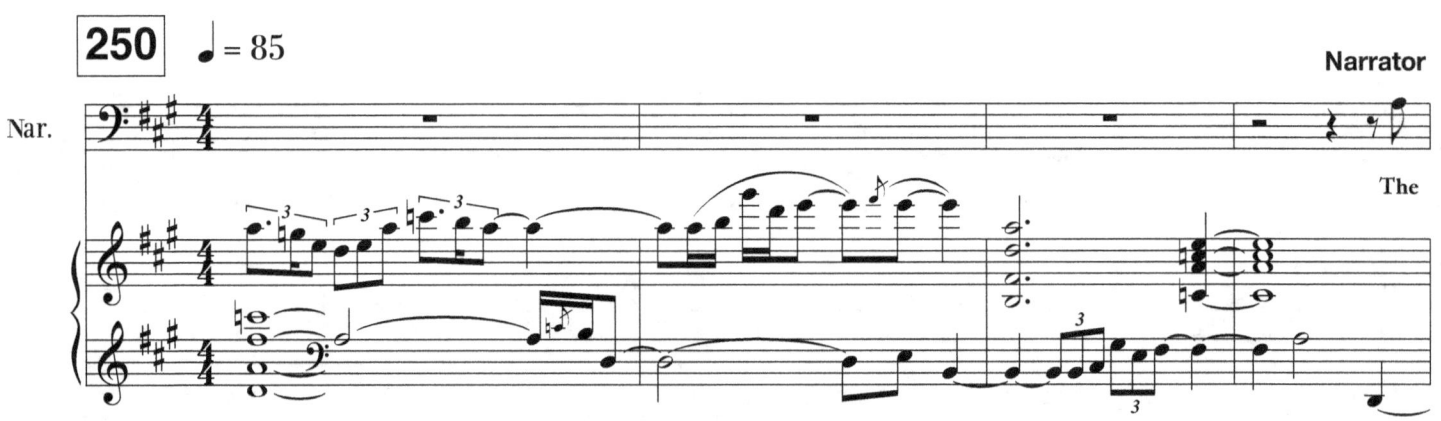

Nar. The

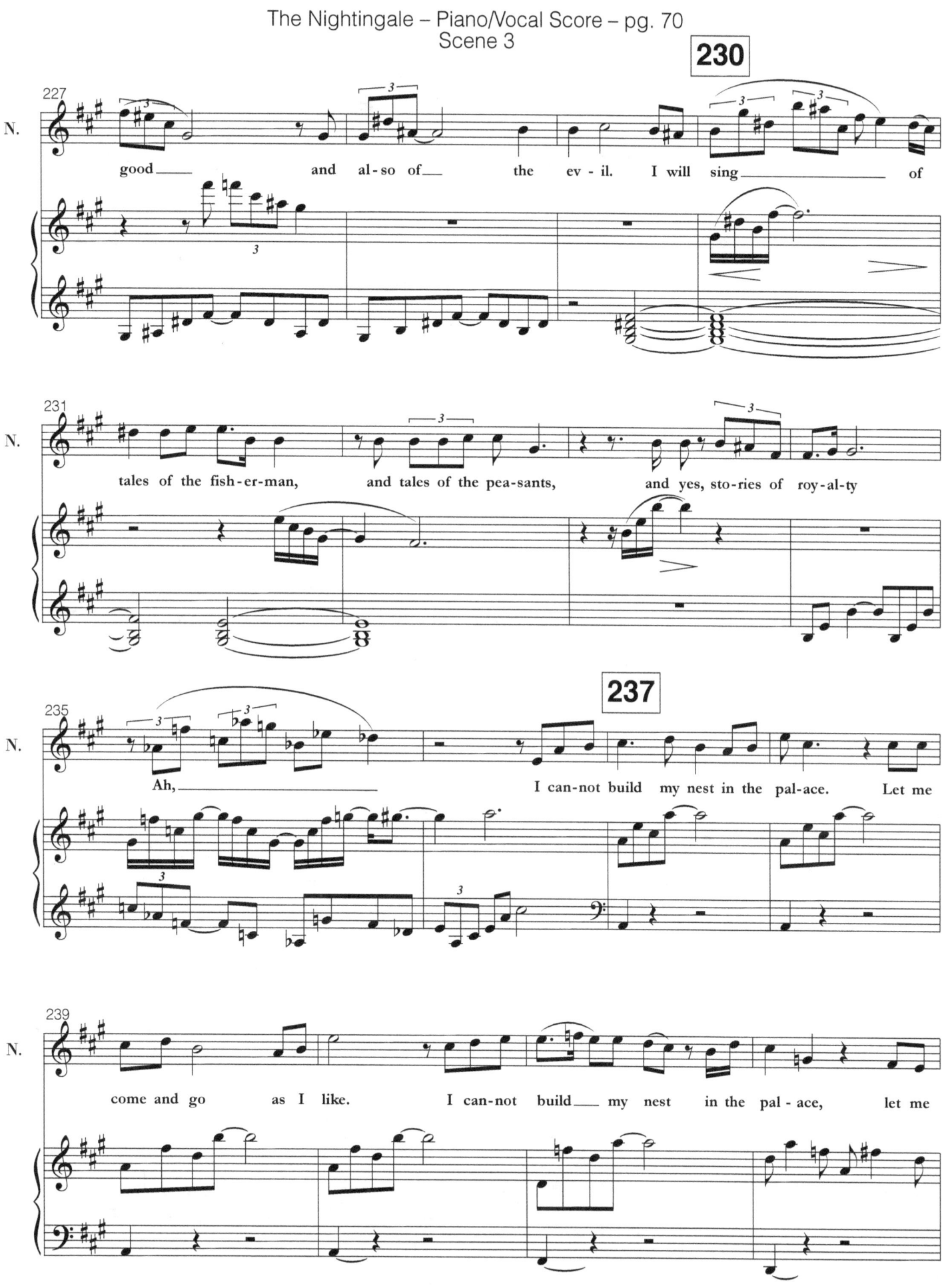

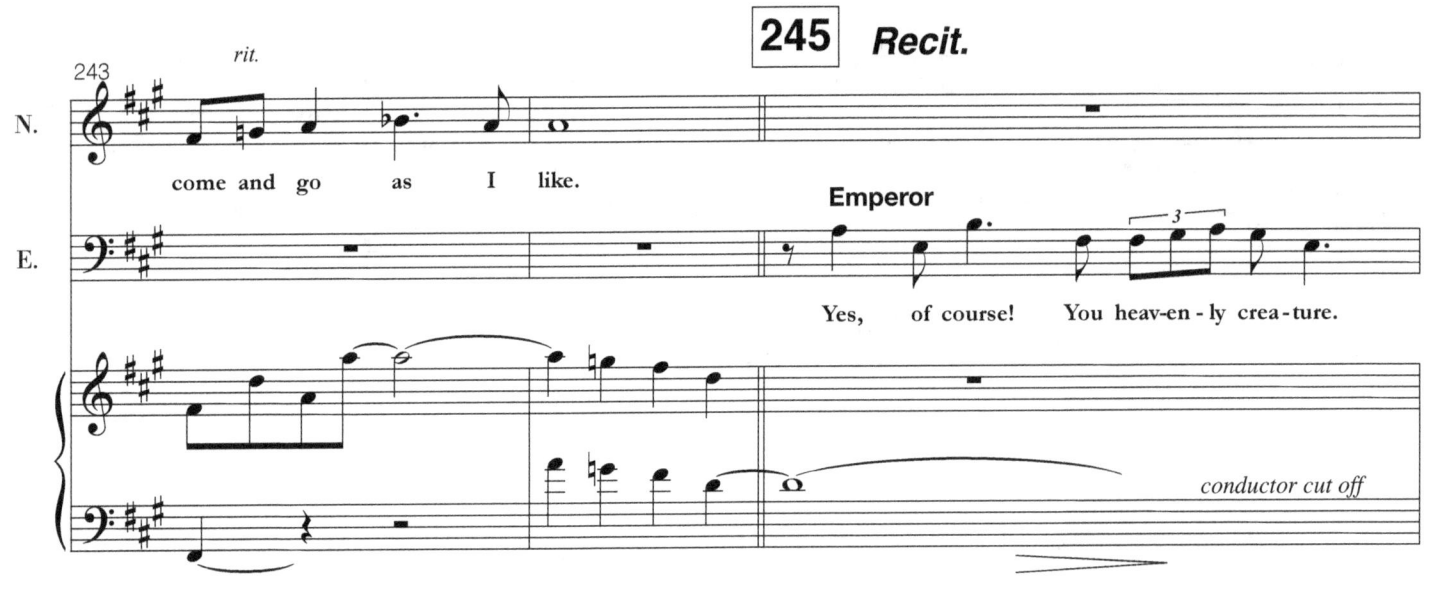

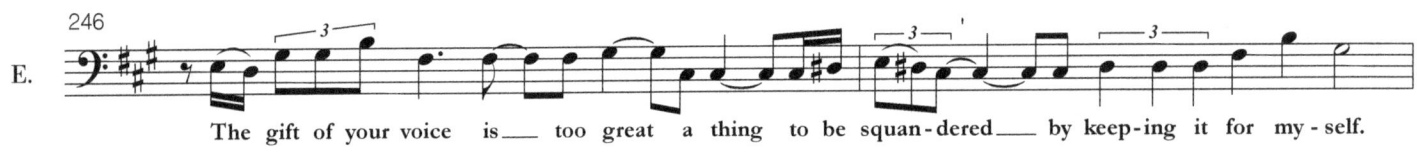

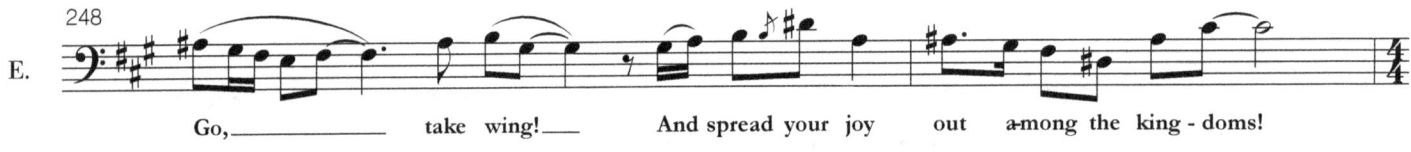

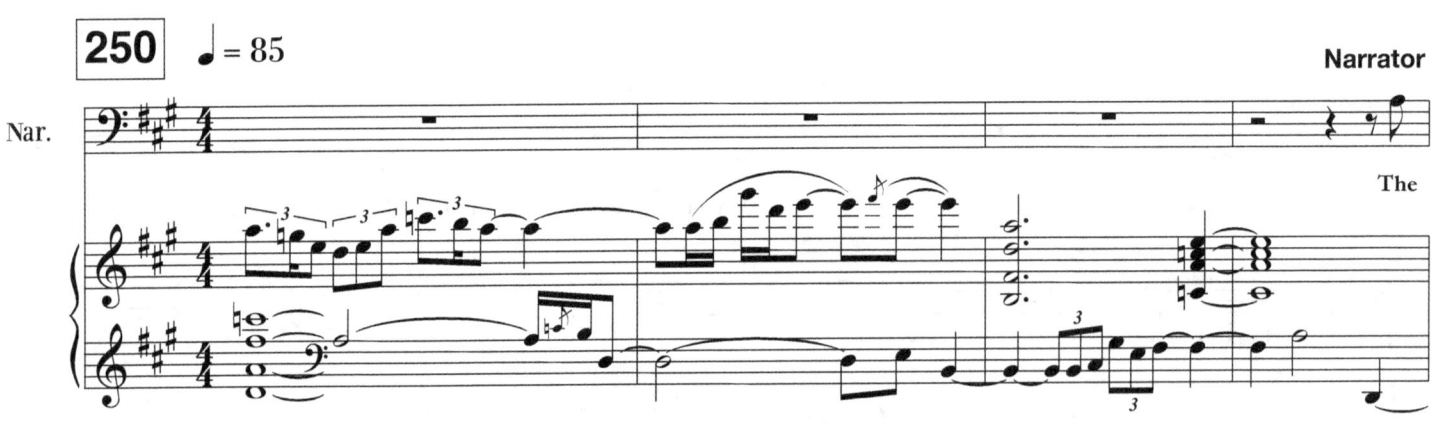

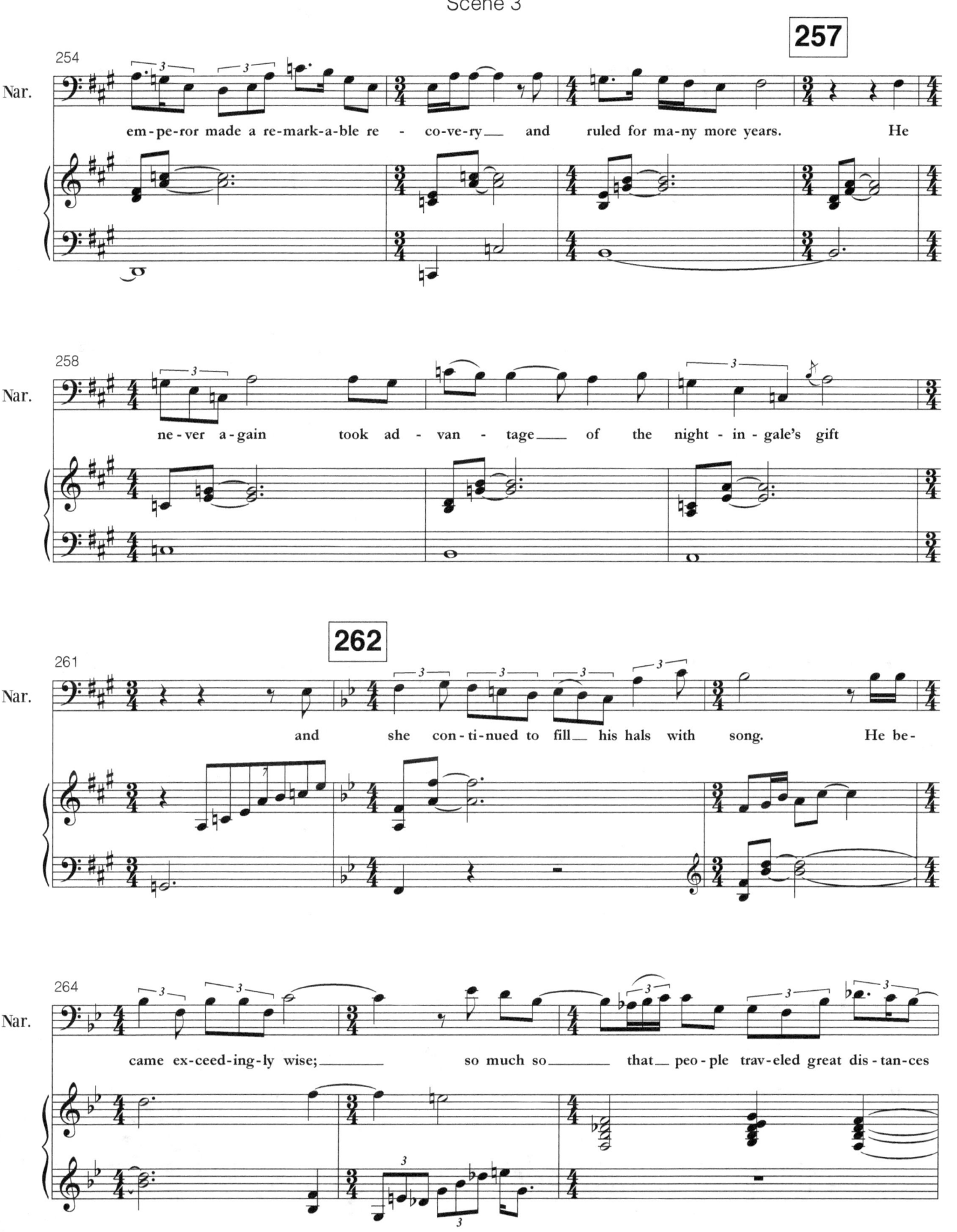

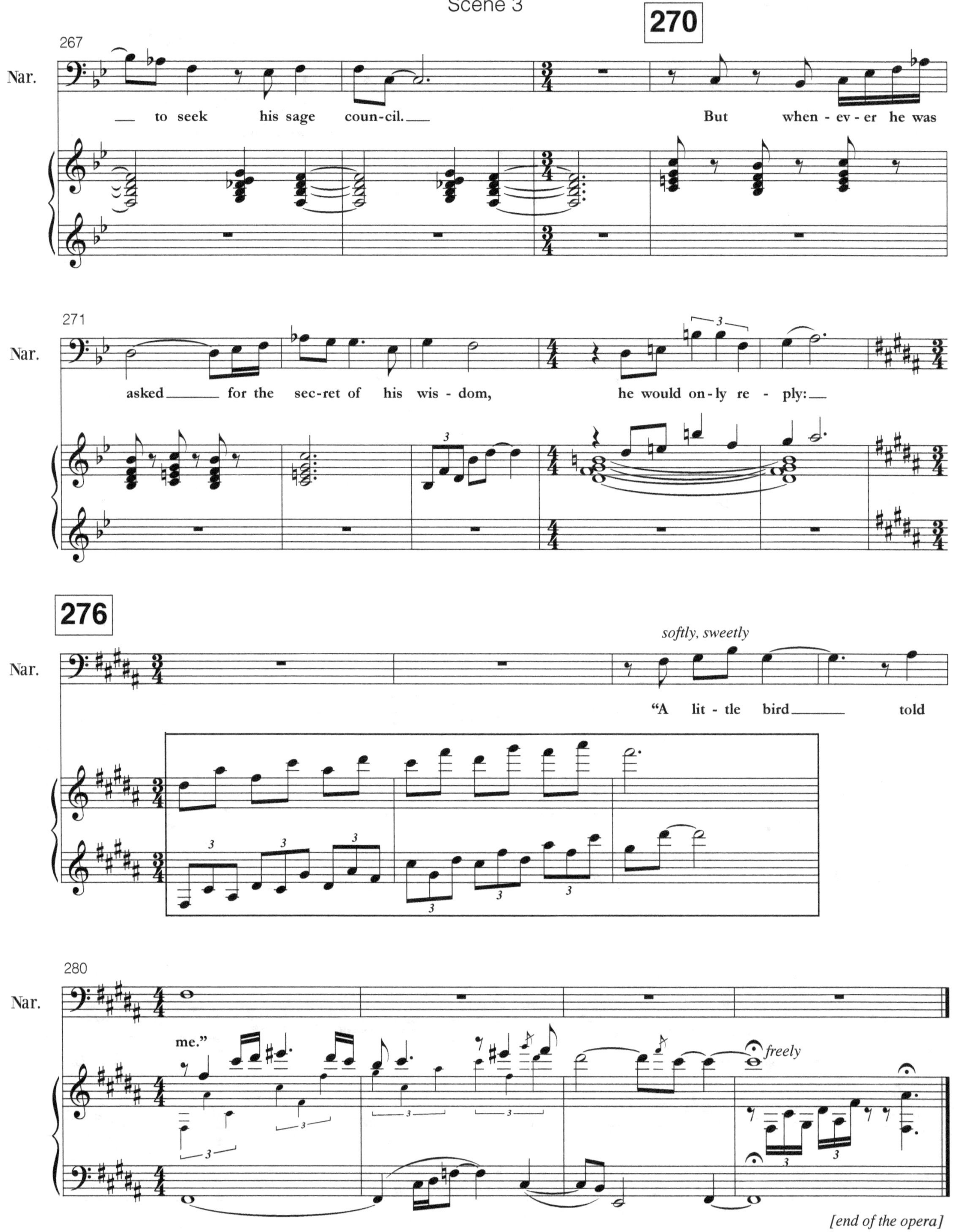

[end of the opera]